175 Pound Cake Recipes

(175 Pound Cake Recipes - Volume 1)

Tori Ramos

Content

175 Awesome Pound Cake Recipes

***

---
1. 5 Flavor (Pound Cake) Cupcakes

Serving: 2-3 dozen, 24 serving(s) | Prep: 25mins | Ready in:

Ingredients

- 1 cup butter, softened
- 1/2 cup shortening
- 3 cups sugar
- 5 eggs, beaten, at room temperature
- 3 cups flour
- 1/2 teaspoon baking powder
- 1 cup milk
- 1 teaspoon coconut, flavor
- 1 teaspoon rum, flavor
- 1 teaspoon butter flavor extract
- 1 teaspoon lemon extract
- 1 teaspoon vanilla extract
- 6 Flavor Glaze
- 1 cup sugar
- 1/2 cup water
- 1 teaspoon coconut
- 1 teaspoon rum
- 1 teaspoon butter
- 1 teaspoon lemon extract
- 1 teaspoon vanilla
- 1 teaspoon almond extract

Direction

- Preheat oven to 325.
- Cream butter, shortening, and sugar until light and fluffy.
- Beat eggs until they are lemon colored, add to the butter mixture.
- Combine flour and baking powder, add to the creamed mixture alternately with milk.
- Stir in flavorings. Beat on high speed 1 minute.
- Line muffin pans with paper baking cups and fill 2/3 full. Tap pan a few times to remove air bubbles.
- Bake at 325 for 20 minutes.
- Make Glaze:
- Combine ingredients in heavy saucepan. Bring to a boil, stirring until sugar is melted.
- Pour half of glaze over the cupcakes while they are still in the pan, then the other half after they are removed.

Nutrition Information

- Calories: 318.4
- Total Fat: 13.7
- Saturated Fat: 6.6
- Sodium: 83.2
- Sugar: 33.5
- Cholesterol: 66.2
- Fiber: 0.4
- Total Carbohydrate: 45.9
- Protein: 3.3

---
2. Addie's Pound Cake

Serving: 1 Cake, 16 serving(s) | Prep: 10mins | Ready in:

Ingredients

- 1 cup butter
- 3 cups sugar
- 6 eggs
- 3 cups flour
- 1/2 pint whipping cream
- 1 teaspoon vanilla extract
- 1 teaspoon lemon extract

Direction

- Cream butter and sugar. Add eggs one at a time. Sift flour three times. Add flour and whipping cream alternately to butter mixture. Add extracts. Grease steeple pan. Bake on middle rack for 1 1/2 hours at 350 degrees.
- Cool for 15 minutes then invert pan.

Nutrition Information

- Calories: 411.7
- Protein: 5.2
- Saturated Fat: 11.3
- Sugar: 37.6
- Cholesterol: 120.6
- Total Fat: 19
- Sodium: 134.4
- Fiber: 0.6
- Total Carbohydrate: 56

3. Almond Poppy Seed Pound Cake

Serving: 1 loaf, 8-10 serving(s) | Prep: 30mins | Ready in:

Ingredients

- 1 1/2 cups all-purpose flour
- 1/4 teaspoon baking soda
- 1/4 teaspoon salt
- 3/4 cup butter, at room temperature, plus extra for greasing
- 1 cup sugar
- 1 1/2 teaspoons vanilla extract
- 1/2 teaspoon almond extract
- 2 large eggs
- 1/2 cup sour cream
- 0.5 (8 ounce) can poppy seed filling

Direction

- Preheat oven to 325°F Lightly grease an 8 1/2 by 4 1/2 loaf pan.
- In a bowl, mix the flour, baking soda, and salt and set aside.
- In another bowl beat together the butter, sugar, vanilla, and almond extract until light and fluffy. Add the eggs one at a time beating well after each addition, until just blended.
- Sprinkle half the four mixture into the egg mixture and stir until just incorporated. Stir in the sour cream, then sprinkle in the rest of the flour mixture.
- Add the Poppy filling until just incorporated.
- Pour the batter into prepared pan and tap. Bake until toothpick inserted in the middle comes out clean, about 70 minutes, or longer if using a metal pan. Let cool 15 minutes.
- Run a knife around the inside of the pan, invert the cake onto a wire rack, and lift off the pan.
- Serve warm or at room temperature.

Nutrition Information

- Calories: 433.9
- Total Fat: 23
- Sodium: 270.8
- Sugar: 25.3
- Total Carbohydrate: 52
- Cholesterol: 105
- Protein: 5.3
- Saturated Fat: 13.4
- Fiber: 0.6

4. Almond Ricotta Pound Cake

Serving: 1 loaf, 12 serving(s) | Prep: 15mins | Ready in:

Ingredients

- 1 1/2 cups flour
- 3 teaspoons baking powder
- 1 teaspoon salt
- 1 1/2 cups sugar
- 3/4 cup unsalted butter
- 1 cup ricotta cheese

- 1/2 cup cream cheese
- 3 large eggs
- 1 teaspoon lemon juice
- 2 teaspoons vanilla extract
- 1 tablespoon almond extract

Direction

- Preheat the oven to 350 degrees.
- Grease a 9x5 loaf pan.
- Combine the flour, baking powder, salt, and sugar.
- Add in the butter and mix with a hand mixer.
- Mix in the ricotta cheese, cream cheese, and eggs.
- Mix in the lemon juice, vanilla extract, and almond extract.
- Pour batter in the loaf pan. Bake for around 50 minutes.

Nutrition Information

- Calories: 347.8
- Total Fat: 18.8
- Sodium: 352.9
- Fiber: 0.4
- Cholesterol: 98.1
- Saturated Fat: 11.3
- Sugar: 25.6
- Total Carbohydrate: 38.6
- Protein: 6.2

5. American Kitchen Classic Basic Pound Cake

Serving: 8 serving(s) | Prep: 15mins | Ready in:

Ingredients

- 1 cup unsalted butter, slightly firm
- 1 tablespoon unsalted butter, softened
- 1 3/4 cups all-purpose flour, sifted
- 1/2 teaspoon table salt
- 5 large eggs

- 1 1/2 teaspoons pure vanilla extract
- 1 1/4 cups superfine sugar
- powdered sugar, for dusting

Direction

- Position a rack in the center of the oven and heat the oven to 325 degrees F. Using a pastry brush, thoroughly coat an 8-1/2 x 4-1/2 x 2-3/4-inch loaf pan with 1 tbsp. softened butter. Line the bottom with a rectangle of parchment.
- In a medium bowl, combine the flour and salt and whisk thoroughly.
- Using a stand mixer fitted with the whisk attachment, beat the eggs on medium-high speed until thickened and lightened in color, 3 to 4 minutes. Transfer to a medium bowl and set aside. Clean the bowl of the stand mixer and fit it with the paddle attachment.
- Beat the butter on medium-low speed until smooth and creamy, 1 to 2 minutes. Add the vanilla extract and mix 1 minute longer. Add the sugar 1 to 2 tbsp. at a time, taking about 4 minutes to add it all and scraping the bowl as needed.
- Still on medium-low speed, slowly add half of the beaten eggs, taking about 2 minutes to add them. Scrape the bowl as needed and beat for 30 seconds more.
- Reduce the speed to low and add the dry ingredients alternately with the remaining eggs (divide the flour into 3 parts and the eggs into 2 parts), mixing just until each addition is incorporated. Scrape the bowl and beat on medium low for 10 seconds more.
- Spoon the batter into the prepared pan. Smooth the top with the back of a large soup spoon, making sure to reach well into the corners. Bang the pan on the counter two times to remove any air pockets.
- Bake the cake until the top is golden-brown, the sides begin to pull away from the pan, and a thin wooden skewer inserted slightly off center into the cake (not into the crack) comes out clean, 1 hour and 20 to 25 minutes.
- During the last 15 minutes of baking, lightly spray a 12-inch strip of aluminum foil with

nonstick cooking spray and rest it loosely on top of the cake. Transfer to a wire rack and let cool for at least 20 minutes before removing from the pan.
- Dust the top with confectioners' sugar and use a serrated knife to cut the cake into 1/2-inch slices.

Nutrition Information

- Calories: 483.6
- Total Carbohydrate: 52.5
- Cholesterol: 181.1
- Protein: 7
- Sodium: 194
- Fiber: 0.7
- Sugar: 31.5
- Total Fat: 27.7
- Saturated Fat: 16.5

6. Antoinette's Plain Pound Cake (W/ Crisco)

Serving: 10 serving(s) | Prep: 15mins | Ready in:

Ingredients

- 1 cup Crisco
- 4 beaten eggs
- 2 cups sugar
- 2 teaspoons vanilla
- 3 cups flour
- 3 teaspoons baking powder
- 1 cup milk

Direction

- Cream together Crisco and sugar. Add eggs and vanilla.
- Sift flour and baking powder together and add to egg mixture along with milk.
- Bake in a tube pan at 350 for one hour.

Nutrition Information

- Calories: 520.7
- Total Fat: 23.8
- Saturated Fat: 7.5
- Fiber: 1
- Sugar: 40.3
- Total Carbohydrate: 70.3
- Protein: 7.2
- Sodium: 149.7
- Cholesterol: 88

7. Apricot Brandy Pound Cake

Serving: 15 serving(s) | Prep: 30mins | Ready in:

Ingredients

- 3 cups sugar
- 1 cup margarine
- 6 eggs
- 3 cups flour
- 1/4 teaspoon baking soda
- 1/2 teaspoon salt
- 1 cup sour cream
- 1/2 cup apricot brandy
- 1 teaspoon orange extract
- 1 teaspoon pure vanilla extract
- 1/2 teaspoon rum extract
- 1/2 teaspoon lemon extract
- 1/2 teaspoon almond extract

Direction

- Grease and flour a very large tube pan.
- Cream together sugar and butter add eggs one at a time.
- Mix dry things and set aside.
- Mix sour cream and all flavorings and brandy.
- Alternately add dry and wet to sugar mix.
- Mix until well blended then pour into pan and bake at 325 for 70 minutes.

Nutrition Information

- Calories: 418.9
- Sugar: 40.3
- Cholesterol: 91.3
- Protein: 5.7
- Fiber: 0.7
- Total Carbohydrate: 60.1
- Total Fat: 17.6
- Saturated Fat: 4.8
- Sodium: 277

8. Audrey's Lite Lemon Pound Cake

Serving: 12 serving(s) | Prep: 10mins | Ready in:

Ingredients

- 8 ounces low-fat cream cheese, softened
- 3⁄4 cup skim milk
- 1 (1 ounce) package sugar-free instant lemon pudding
- 1 (18 1/4 ounce) box lemon cake mix
- 4 eggs or 4 cups egg substitute
- Optional Glaze
- 1 cup confectioners' sugar (optional)
- 2 2⁄3 tablespoons lemon juice (freshly squeezed is best) (optional)
- sliced strawberry (optional)
- whipped topping (optional)

Direction

- In a mixing bowl, beat cream cheese until smooth; gradually beat in milk and pudding.
- Add dry cakes mix and eggs; beat until combined.
- Beat on medium speed for 2 minutes.
- Pour into a greased and floured 10" fluted tube pan.
- Bake at 350 degrees for 40- 45 minutes or until a toothpick inserted comes out clean.
- Cool for 10 minutes before removing from pan to a wire rack to cool completely.

Nutrition Information

- Calories: 266.2
- Cholesterol: 86
- Sodium: 391.1
- Sugar: 18.8
- Total Carbohydrate: 35.2
- Total Fat: 11.1
- Saturated Fat: 4.1
- Fiber: 0.5
- Protein: 6.5

9. Baillio's Quick And Moist Pound Cake

Serving: 1 Cake, 12 serving(s) | Prep: 10mins | Ready in:

Ingredients

- 1 package yellow cake mix
- 1⁄2 cup oil
- 1 cup water
- 4 eggs
- 1 can coconut pecan frosting

Direction

- Mix all ingredients together, including the frosting.
- Bake at 325° for 1 hour.

Nutrition Information

- Calories: 460.1
- Cholesterol: 71.4
- Sodium: 385.7
- Fiber: 1.4
- Sugar: 34.5
- Total Carbohydrate: 54.5
- Protein: 4.6
- Total Fat: 25.1
- Saturated Fat: 5.8

10. Banana Cream Cheese Pound Cake

Serving: 20 serving(s) | Prep: 20mins | Ready in:

Ingredients

- 1 (8 ounce) package cream cheese (softened)
- 2 cups butter (softened)
- 3 cups sugar (sifted)
- 3 bananas (softened and slightly brown)
- 3 cups cake flour (without salt and baking powder)
- 3 teaspoons baking powder
- 3 teaspoons pure vanilla extract
- 6 large eggs (room temperature)

Direction

- Preheat oven to 350 degrees.
- Add Butter, Sugar and Cream Cheese to mixing bowl and mix until smooth and creamy (60 sec).
- Mash the Bananas then add to the mixing bowl and mix well (15 sec).
- Add Vanilla Extract to the mixing bowl and mix well (15 sec).
- Add Eggs one at a time, ensure that each Egg is mixed well before adding the next Egg (10 sec per egg).
- Sift the Cake Flour and Baking Powder together.
- Add Cake Flour/Baking Powder into the mixing bowl and mix well until the mixture is smooth throughout (90 sec).
- Grease and Flour at tube pan 10-in or 12-in.
- Pour cake mixture to pan, put pan into oven and immediately reduce heat to 325 degrees.
- Bake cake at 325 degrees for 1 hour and 30 minutes or until a wooden tester comes out clean.
- Cool in pan for 10 minutes, then cool on wire rack.
- Serve with Vanilla Bean Ice Cream and enjoy!

Nutrition Information

- Calories: 431.5
- Sodium: 275.2
- Sugar: 32.7
- Total Carbohydrate: 50.9
- Cholesterol: 117.1
- Saturated Fat: 14.4
- Protein: 4.6
- Total Fat: 24
- Fiber: 0.8

11. Banana Pound Cake With A Caramel Glaze

Serving: 16 serving(s) | Prep: 15mins | Ready in:

Ingredients

- 3 cups flour
- 1/2 teaspoon baking powder
- 1/2 teaspoon baking soda
- 1/2 teaspoon salt
- 1 cup butter, softened
- 1/2 cup shortening
- 2 cups packed light brown sugar
- 1 cup sugar
- 5 large eggs
- 1/2 cup milk
- 1 banana, mashed
- 1 cup chopped pecans
- 2 teaspoons vanilla extract
- CARAMEL GLAZE
- 1/4 cup butter, softened
- 1/4 cup packed light brown sugar
- 1/4 cup sugar
- 1/4 cup whipping cream
- 1 teaspoon vanilla extract

Direction

- Preheat the oven to 325°F.
- Mix the flour, baking powder, baking soda and salt together.

- Cream the butter and shortening together, then beat in the brown and white sugars gradually, beating constantly for 5 to 7 minutes. Add the eggs one at a time, beating until the yellow disappears.
- Add the flour mixture alternately with the milk, beating at low speed until blended after each addition, beginning and ending with the flour mixture.
- Stir in the banana, pecans and vanilla. Pour into a greased and floured 10 inch tube pan.
- Bake for 65 minutes or until a wooden pick inserted in the center comes out clean. Cool on a wire rack for 10 minutes before removing from the pan to cool completely on a wire rack.
- To make the glaze, bring the butter, brown sugar, white sugar and cream to a boil in a heavy saucepan over high heat, stirring frequently. Boil for 1 minute, without stirring. Remove from the heat. Stir in the Vanilla. Cool until slightly thickened, then drizzle over the cooled cake.

Nutrition Information

- Calories: 543.2
- Sodium: 286.7
- Fiber: 1.5
- Sugar: 47
- Total Carbohydrate: 67.2
- Cholesterol: 102.4
- Protein: 5.6
- Total Fat: 29.1
- Saturated Fat: 12.7

12. Banana Nut Pound Cake

Serving: 12 serving(s) | Prep: 20mins | Ready in:

Ingredients

- 3 1/4 cups all-purpose flour
- 1/2 teaspoon baking powder
- 1/2 teaspoon salt
- 1 (8 ounce) package cream cheese, softened
- 1/2 cup butter, softened
- 3 cups sugar
- 4 eggs
- 2 medium bananas, mashed (about 1 cup)
- 1/4 cup Bourbon or 1/4 cup low-fat milk
- 1 tablespoon vanilla
- 1 cup chopped pecans, toasted
- powdered sugar

Direction

- Preheat oven to 325 degrees. Grease and flour a 10-inch fluted tube pan; set aside.
- In a bowl combine flour, baking powder and salt; set aside.
- In a large mixing bowl beat cream cheese and butter with an electric mixer on medium speed until combined. Gradually add sugar, beating about 7 minutes or until light.
- Add eggs, one at a time, beating 1 minute after each addition; scrape bowl frequently.
- In a separate bowl combine bananas, bourbon and vanilla. Alternately add flour mixture and banana mixture to butter mixture; beat on low to medium speed after each addition just until combined. Stir in pecans. Spread evenly into prepared pan.
- Bake 80 minutes or until a toothpick inserted near center comes out clean. Cool cake in pan on a wire rack for 10 minutes. Remove from pan; cool on rack.
- Sprinkle with powdered sugar. To acquire an even sprinkling, use a sieve.

Nutrition Information

- Calories: 570.3
- Total Fat: 22.7
- Sugar: 53.6
- Total Carbohydrate: 82.7
- Cholesterol: 103.2
- Protein: 7.8
- Saturated Fat: 9.7
- Sodium: 265.5

- Fiber: 2.3

13. Basic Pound Cake.

Serving: 12 serving(s) | Prep: 15mins | Ready in:

Ingredients

- 1/2 lb flour (any type of white flour)
- 1/2 lb egg (weigh eggs with their shells)
- 1/2 lb soft butter
- 1/2 lb sugar
- 1 teaspoon vanilla extract
- 1 pinch salt
- 2 teaspoons baking powder

Direction

- Preheat oven to 350°.
- Add all the ingredients to a bowl of a cake mixer.
- Beat on high for 7 minutes.
- Grease a loaf dish.
- Pour cake batter into dish.
- Bake for 65 minutes; check doneness with toothpick or cake tester.
- Allow to cool covered with paper towel for 30 minutes.
- Transfer to cooling rack and allow to cool covered.
- Once cooled, cut into slices and serve.

Nutrition Information

- Calories: 306.1
- Total Fat: 17.3
- Saturated Fat: 10.3
- Fiber: 0.5
- Sodium: 236
- Sugar: 19
- Total Carbohydrate: 33.7
- Cholesterol: 111
- Protein: 4.5

14. Best Pound Cake

Serving: 18 serving(s) | Prep: 15mins | Ready in:

Ingredients

- 1 cup unsalted butter
- 1/2 cup shortening
- 3 cups granulated sugar
- 5 eggs
- 3 cups ap flour
- 1/2 teaspoon salt
- 1/2 teaspoon baking powder
- 1 cup whole milk
- 1 teaspoon vanilla

Direction

- For Bundt: preheat oven to 350°F.
- For muffins: preheat to 325°F.
- Combine the dry ingredients together in a bowl and set aside. Cream the shortening and butter together in a large mixing bowl while slowly adding sugar. Next add eggs one at a time while continuing to mix. Now add some flour and some milk, keep mixing, add some more flour, then milk, keep mixing, add the milk and then flour and mix. Now add in the vanilla. Pour the ingredients into a greased and floured pan of your choice.
- For Bundt: bake 60 - 90 min (check with toothpick for doneness).
- For muffins: 40 - 60 min (again, check with a toothpick).
- Enjoy.

Nutrition Information

- Calories: 374.8
- Fiber: 0.6
- Total Carbohydrate: 50
- Cholesterol: 87.2
- Protein: 4.4
- Total Fat: 17.9
- Saturated Fat: 8.6

- Sugar: 34.2
- Sodium: 101.4

---

15. Bittersweet Chocolate Pound Cake With Decadent Glaze

Serving: 12 serving(s) | Prep: 20mins | Ready in:

Ingredients

- Cake
- 6 ounces unsweetened baking chocolate, melted
- 2 cups flour
- 1 teaspoon baking soda
- 1 teaspoon baking powder
- 2 tablespoons instant coffee
- 2 tablespoons hot water
- cold water
- 2 cups sugar
- 1 cup butter, softened
- 1 teaspoon vanilla
- 3 eggs
- Dark Chocolate Glaze
- 2 ounces unsweetened baking chocolate
- 3 tablespoons butter
- 1 1/2 cups confectioners' sugar
- 3 -4 tablespoons water
- 1 teaspoon vanilla

Direction

- CAKE: Preheat oven to 325 degrees.
- Grease and flour a Bundt or tube pan.
- In a small bowl, combine flour, soda and powder.
- In a 2 cup measuring cup, dissolve coffee in hot water and add enough cold water to measure 1 1/2 cups.
- In a large mixer bowl, beat granulated sugar, butter and vanilla until creamy.
- Beat in eggs, one at a time.
- Stir in melted chocolate.
- Add flour mixture alternately with coffee mixture.
- Pour into prepared pan.
- Bake 1 hour or until center tests done.
- Cool 30 minutes and remove from pan onto a wire rack.
- Cool completely and transfer to serving dish.
- Drizzle with glaze and sprinkle with confectioner's sugar, if desired.
- GLAZE: Melt chocolate and butter, stirring until smooth.
- Remove from heat and stir in confectioner's sugar, alternately with water, until desired consistency is reached.
- Stir in vanilla extract.

Nutrition Information

- Calories: 543.9
- Saturated Fat: 18.2
- Sodium: 287.8
- Fiber: 3.8
- Total Fat: 29.8
- Sugar: 48.4
- Total Carbohydrate: 70.6
- Cholesterol: 101.2
- Protein: 6.5

---

16. Black Forest Pound Cake

Serving: 10 serving(s) | Prep: 40mins | Ready in:

Ingredients

- 2/3 cup butter, softened
- 1 1/3 cups granulated sugar
- 2/3 cup brown sugar, firmly packed
- 4 large eggs
- 1 1/4 teaspoons vanilla extract, divided
- 1 1/2 cups cake flour
- 1/2 cup unsweetened cocoa
- 1/2 teaspoon salt
- 1/4 teaspoon baking soda
- 3/4 cup sour cream

- 3 ounces bittersweet chocolate squares, finely chopped
- 2 (12 ounce) packages frozen cherries
- 1/3 cup sugar
- 1/3 cup cold water
- 2 teaspoons cornstarch
- 2 tablespoons kirsch or 2 tablespoons brandy
- 1/2 teaspoon vanilla extract
- 1 pinch salt
- 1 1/4 cups heavy cream
- 1 tablespoon granulated sugar
- shaved bittersweet chocolate

Direction

- Preheat oven to 325°. Beat butter at medium speed with a heavy-duty electric stand mixer until creamy. Gradually add 1 1/3 cups granulated sugar and 2/3 cup brown sugar, beating until light and fluffy (about 5 minutes). Add eggs, 1 at a time, beating just until blended after each addition. Beat in 1 teaspoons vanilla.
- Whisk together flour, cocoa, 1/2 tsp salt and baking soda. Add to butter mixture alternately with sour cream, beginning and ending with flour mixture. Beat at low speed just until blended after each addition. Stir in chopped chocolate. Pour batter into a greased and floured 10-inch round cake pan (with sides that are 3 inches high). Bake at 325° for 1 hour and 10 minutes to 1 hour and 20 minutes or until a wooden pick inserted in center comes out clean. Cool in pan on a wire rack 15 minutes. Remove from pan to wire rack; cool completely (about 1 hour).
- Meanwhile, prepare Cherry Sauce. Stir together cherries, sugar, cold water, and cornstarch in a medium saucepan. Cook over medium low heat, stirring often, 12 to 15 minutes or until thickened. Remove from heat, and stir in Kirsch or brandy, vanilla, and salt. Cool completely (about 1 hour).
- Place cake on a serving plate or cake stand. Slowly pour Cherry Sauce over cake. Beat heavy cream, 1 tablespoons granulated sugar, and remaining 1/4 teaspoons vanilla at

medium-high speed until soft peaks form. Dollop whipped cream onto cake, and sprinkle with shaved chocolate.

Nutrition Information

- Calories: 611.6
- Sugar: 63.5
- Cholesterol: 156.7
- Total Fat: 29.4
- Sodium: 331.6
- Fiber: 3.2
- Protein: 6.9
- Saturated Fat: 17.6
- Total Carbohydrate: 84.8

17. Black Walnut Pound Cake With Frosting

Serving: 12-16 serving(s) | Prep: 20mins | Ready in:

Ingredients

- Cake
- 1 cup butter
- 1/2 cup shortening
- 3 cups sugar
- 5 eggs
- 1 cup sour cream
- 1/2 teaspoon baking powder
- 3 cups cake flour or 3 cups plain flour
- 1/2 cup milk
- 1 tablespoon vanilla flavoring
- 1 tablespoon black walnut flavoring
- 1 cup black walnut, chopped
- Frosting
- 1/4 cup butter
- 4 ounces cream cheese
- 1 tablespoon black walnut flavoring
- 1 lb powdered sugar
- 1/2 cup black walnut, chopped
- milk, if needed

Direction

- Oven at 325° F.
- Cake:
- Cream butter and shortening.
- Add sugar and cream together.
- Add eggs 1 at a time, beating well after each.
- Add sour cream and mix together.
- Add baking powder to flour.
- Add to creamed mixture, alternating flour mixture and milk.
- Add flavorings and mix well.
- Mix in chopped black walnuts by hand.
- Pour into a greased and floured 10 inch tube pan.
- Bake for 1 hour, turn down oven to 300°F for 30 minutes more.
- Remove and cool.
- Frosting:
- Cream butter and cream cheese.
- Add flavoring and powdered sugar.
- Mix nuts in by hand. Mix well.
- Put on cooled cake.

Nutrition Information

- Calories: 919.8
- Cholesterol: 159.2
- Total Fat: 47
- Total Carbohydrate: 117.7
- Sugar: 87.5
- Protein: 11
- Saturated Fat: 20.3
- Sodium: 225
- Fiber: 1.6

18. Blueberry Pound Cake On The Grill

Serving: 6 serving(s) | Prep: 10mins | Ready in:

Ingredients

- 1/3 cup sugar
- 2 tablespoons butter
- 1 ounce fat free cream cheese
- 1 egg
- 3⁄4 cup flour, divided (I used 1/4 white wheat)
- 1⁄2 cup blueberries (fresh or frozen)
- 1⁄4 teaspoon baking powder
- 1⁄8 teaspoon baking soda
- 1⁄8 teaspoon salt
- 1⁄4 cup non-fat vanilla yogurt
- 1⁄2 teaspoon vanilla extract

Direction

- Preheat grill to 350. Leave at least one burner off, as you will want to bake this with indirect heat.
- Beat first 3 ingredients at medium speed until well blended. Add egg and beat again.
- Combine flour (less 2 T) with baking powder, baking soda, and salt.
- Combine remaining 2 T flour with blueberries and toss to coat.
- Add flour mixture to sugar mixture then add yogurt.
- Fold in blueberry mixture and vanilla.
- Spray an 8-inch cast iron skillet well with cooking spray and pour the batter into the pan. Cover with foil but tent well as the batter will rise.
- Place pan on grill, above whichever burner you have left turned off. Alternatively you might be able to use a higher rack on your grill but I have not tried this.
- Bake 30 minutes and check, then bake another 15 minutes or so (until a fork inserted in the center comes out clean). Enjoy!

Nutrition Information

- Calories: 158.8
- Cholesterol: 41.7
- Total Fat: 4.9
- Fiber: 0.7
- Sugar: 12.7
- Saturated Fat: 2.8
- Sodium: 169.2

- Total Carbohydrate: 25.3
- Protein: 3.5

19. Bobbie's Pound Cake

Serving: 10 serving(s) | Prep: 15mins | Ready in:

Ingredients

- 1 cup butter
- 1/2 cup Crisco
- 3 cups sugar
- 5 large eggs
- 3 cups flour
- 1 cup milk
- 2 tablespoons vanilla

Direction

- Do not preheat oven.
- Cream together the butter, Crisco and sugar.
- Add eggs one at a time.
- Beat well after each egg.
- Add alternately the flour, milk and vanilla.
- Mix well after each addition.
- Grease and flour a Bundt pan.
- Put in cold over, turn the oven to 350
- Cook at 350 one hour and 20 minutes.

Nutrition Information

- Calories: 681.9
- Total Fat: 32.4
- Fiber: 1
- Cholesterol: 158
- Saturated Fat: 16.2
- Sodium: 178.7
- Sugar: 60.6
- Total Carbohydrate: 90.3
- Protein: 8

20. Bourbon Brown Sugar Pound Cake

Serving: 1 cake | Prep: 25mins | Ready in:

Ingredients

- 3 cups flour
- 3/4 teaspoon salt
- 1/2 teaspoon baking powder
- 1/2 teaspoon baking soda
- 3/4 cup whole milk
- 2 teaspoons vanilla extract
- 4 tablespoons Bourbon
- 1 1/2 cups dark brown sugar, packed
- 1/2 cup sugar
- 1 cup butter, softened (2 sticks)
- 5 eggs
- FROSTING
- 2 tablespoons orange juice
- 1/3 cup sugar
- 2 tablespoons Bourbon
- strawberry (to garnish)
- blueberries (to garnish)

Direction

- Preheat oven to 325°F.
- Grease and flour a 12-cup Bundt pan.
- In a medium bowl, combine flour, salt, baking powder, and baking soda.
- Combine the milk, vanilla, and 4 tablespoons bourbon.
- In large bowl, with mixer at medium speed, beat brown sugar and 1/2 cup sugar until lump free.
- Add butter and beat at high speed until light and creamy, about 5 minutes.
- Add the eggs, one at a time, beating well after each addition.
- At low speed, alternately add flour mixture and milk mixture, beginning and ending with flour mixture.
- Pour batter into prepared pan.
- Bake 1 hour and 20 minutes or until cake springs back when toothpick inserted in center comes out clean.

- Cool cake in pan on a wire rack for 10 minutes.
- Remove cake from pan.
- Frosting:
- In small bowl, combine orange juice, 1/3 cup sugar, and 2 tablespoons bourbon.
- Brush mixture all over warm cake.
- Cool cake completely.
- Garnish with berries or other fruit for a pretty presentation.

Nutrition Information

- Calories: 5643.5
- Total Carbohydrate: 789
- Total Fat: 218.7
- Sodium: 4423.7
- Fiber: 10.2
- Cholesterol: 1563.8
- Protein: 78.2
- Saturated Fat: 128.4
- Sugar: 500.2

21. Bourbon Pound Cake

Serving: 2 cakes, 12-18 serving(s) | Prep: 5mins | Ready in:

Ingredients

- 3 1/2 cups all-purpose flour
- 1 teaspoon baking powder
- 1/2 teaspoon salt
- 1 lb butter, at room temperature
- 2 cups sugar
- 8 large eggs
- 1/3 cup milk (whole milk for best results)
- 1/3 cup Bourbon
- 1 teaspoon vanilla extract

Direction

- Sift the flour, baking powder, and salt together.

- Cream the butter and sugar until light and fluffy.
- Beat in the eggs one at a time.
- Fold in half the flour, then fold in the milk, then the remaining flour, followed by the bourbon and vanilla.
- Pour the batter into two lightly greased and floured 9-inch loaf pans and run the blade of a knife through the batter in an X pattern from corner to corner of the pans to eliminate air bubbles.
- Place the pans in the center of a cool oven, leaving a space between them.
- Turn the oven to 325F and bake for about 1 hour, until a wooden skewer inserted in the middle comes out clean.
- Turn off the oven and let the cakes cool in the oven for 10 minutes.
- Open the oven door and cool for 30 minutes.
- Turn the cakes out onto a wire rack to cool completely before slicing.

Nutrition Information

- Calories: 605.7
- Saturated Fat: 20.7
- Total Fat: 34.6
- Sugar: 33.7
- Total Carbohydrate: 61.9
- Cholesterol: 223.3
- Protein: 8.5
- Sodium: 395.9
- Fiber: 1

22. Bourbon Pecan Pound Cake

Serving: 1 ten-inch cake | Prep: 30mins | Ready in:

Ingredients

- 1 cup shortening
- 2 1/2 cups sugar
- 6 eggs
- 3 cups all-purpose flour

- 2 teaspoons baking powder
- 1/2 teaspoon salt
- 1/2 teaspoon ground nutmeg
- 1 (8 ounce) carton sour cream
- 1/2 cup Bourbon
- 1 cup finely chopped pecans
- Glaze
- 2 1/4 cups sifted powdered sugar
- 2 tablespoons Bourbon
- 2 teaspoons water

Direction

- In a large mixing bowl, cream shortening; gradually add in sugar, beating well using an electric mixer on medium speed.
- Add in eggs, one at a time, beating well after each addition.
- In another bowl, combine flour, baking powder, salt, and nutmeg; set aside.
- In another bowl, combine sour cream and bourbon; add to creamed mixture alternately with flour mixture, beginning and ending with flour mixture.
- Mix just until blended after each addition.
- Fold in pecans.
- Pour batter into a greased/floured 10-inch tube pan.
- Bake in a 325° oven for 1 hour and 10 to 15 minutes or until pick comes out clean.
- Cool cake in pan on a wire rack for 10-15 minutes.
- Remove cake from pan and cool completely on a wire rack.
- In a bowl, combine all the glaze ingredients; stir well.
- Drizzle glaze over cooled cake.

Nutrition Information

- Calories: 8286.9
- Saturated Fat: 99.3
- Total Carbohydrate: 1085.4
- Total Fat: 367.5
- Sugar: 772.2
- Cholesterol: 1374.2

- Protein: 94.1
- Sodium: 2447.6
- Fiber: 20.8

23. Brown Sugar Pound Cake 9x5x3 Inch Loaf Size

Serving: 1 9x5x3-inch loaf, 8 serving(s) | Prep: 10mins | Ready in:

Ingredients

- 1 cup light brown sugar (packed)
- 1 cup butter
- 4 eggs
- 1 teaspoon vanilla extract
- 1 3/4 cups all-purpose flour
- 1/2 teaspoon baking powder
- 1/4 teaspoon salt
- 1 cup toasted chopped pecans (optional)
- sweetened whipped cream (optional)
- assorted berries (optional)

Direction

- Preheat oven to 350F (325F glass or dark loaf pan).
- Grease and flour a 9x5x3-inch loaf pan.
- In a large bowl, beat butter and sugar until light and fluffy.
- Beat in eggs one at a time.
- Add vanilla.
- In a separate bowl, combine flour, baking powder and salt.
- Gradually add flour mixture to sugar mixture.
- If desired, add TOASTED chopped pecans.
- Pour batter into pan.
- (CHECK CAKE AT 55 MINUTES FOR DONENESS) ~ Bake approximately one hour or until a toothpick inserted in center of cake comes out clean.
- Remove from pan and cool completely a wire rack. Serves 8.
- If desired, garnish with whipped cream and assorted berries.

Nutrition Information

- Calories: 444.9
- Sodium: 341.8
- Total Fat: 25.7
- Sugar: 26.9
- Total Carbohydrate: 48.2
- Cholesterol: 154
- Protein: 6.2
- Saturated Fat: 15.4
- Fiber: 0.7

24. Buttercream Pound Cake

Serving: 12 serving(s) | Prep: 20mins | Ready in:

Ingredients

- 1 lb butter, softened (do not use margarine)
- 2 1/2 cups powdered sugar
- 6 eggs
- 2 teaspoons lemon peel, grated
- 3 tablespoons lemon juice
- 4 cups all-purpose flour
- 3 teaspoons baking powder
- 1 (12 1/2 ounce) can poppy seed filling
- 1 cup powdered sugar
- 1 -2 tablespoon lemon juice (or milk)

Direction

- Heat oven to 350°F
- CAKE.
- Beat butter in large bowl until light and fluffy.
- Gradually add 2 1/2 cups powdered sugar, beating until well combined.
- At medium speed, add eggs 1 at a time, beating well after each addition.
- Beat in lemon peel and 3 tablespoons lemon juice.
- Lightly spoon flour into measuring cup; level off.
- At low speed, gradually beat in flour and baking powder; blend well.
- In medium bowl, combine 3 cups batter with poppy seed filling; blend well.
- Spread half of plain batter in bottom of ungreased 10-inch tube pan. Alternately add spoonfuls of poppy seed batter and remaining plain batter.
- Bake at 350°F for 1 hour 15 minutes to 1 hour 25 minutes or until toothpick inserted near center comes out clean.
- Cool 15 minutes; remove from pan. Cool 1 hour or until completely cooled.
- GLAZE.
- In small bowl, combine glaze ingredients, adding enough lemon juice for desired drizzling consistency; blend until smooth. Drizzle over cake.
- High Altitude (3500-6500 ft.), increase flour in cake to 4 1/2 cups. Bake as directed above.

Nutrition Information

- Calories: 695.9
- Saturated Fat: 20.6
- Fiber: 1.2
- Total Carbohydrate: 84.8
- Cholesterol: 187.1
- Total Fat: 36.2
- Sodium: 366.8
- Sugar: 34.7
- Protein: 9.2

25. Cardamom Coffee Pound Cake

Serving: 10 serving(s) | Prep: 15mins | Ready in:

Ingredients

- 1 1/2 cups flour
- 2 teaspoons baking powder
- 1 teaspoon salt
- 1 teaspoon cardamom

- 1 cup plain low-fat yogurt (or 1 cup plain greek yogurt)
- 1 1/4 cups sugar, divided
- 3 eggs
- 1/2 teaspoon vanilla
- 1/2 teaspoon coffee extract (or 1 teaspoon expresso powder dissolved in 1 teaspoon water)
- 1/3 cup olive oil
- 1/4 cup brewed coffee, plus
- 2 tablespoons brewed coffee
- 1 cup powdered sugar

Direction

- Preheat oven to 350 degrees F.
- Grease an 8 1/2 x 4 1/4 inch loaf pan.
- Combine dry ingredients (flour - cardamom).
- In another bowl combine wet ingredients (yogurt, 1 cup sugar - oil) and whisk. Stir in flour mixture.
- Pour batter into prepared pan and bake for 50-55 minutes or until cake tests done with a toothpick or other tester. When cake is done let cool in pan 10 minutes and then place on a wire rack to finish cooling.
- In a saucepan add coffee and remaining 1/4 cup sugar. Heat until sugar dissolves.
- When cake is still warm, poke holes in top of cake and pour coffee mixture over top. Let it soak in and let cake cool.
- To prepare icing: combine powdered sugar, remaining 2 tablespoons of coffee and a pinch of cardamom, stirring until smooth, adding more sugar if necessary to reach spreading consistency. When cake is cool drizzle icing over cake.

Nutrition Information

- Calories: 314.5
- Sodium: 344.9
- Sugar: 38.6
- Total Carbohydrate: 53.5
- Protein: 5.1
- Saturated Fat: 1.7
- Fiber: 0.6
- Cholesterol: 57.3
- Total Fat: 9.2

26. Cheating Lemon Pound Cake

Serving: 1 cake | Prep: 5mins | Ready in:

Ingredients

- 1 (8 ounce) package cream cheese, softened
- 3/4 cup milk
- 1 (18 1/4 ounce) package lemon cake mix
- 4 eggs

Direction

- In mixing bowl, beat cream cheese until smooth. Gradually beat in milk. Add dry cake mix and eggs; beat until combined. Beat on medium speed for 2 minutes.
- Pour into a greased and floured, 1- inch fluted tube pan. Bake at 350°F for 40 to 45 minutes or until a toothpick inserted near centre comes out clean. Cool for 10 minutes before removing from pan. Cool completely on a wire rack.

Nutrition Information

- Calories: 3437.8
- Saturated Fat: 69.2
- Sugar: 226.2
- Protein: 71
- Total Fat: 165.7
- Fiber: 5.7
- Total Carbohydrate: 420.2
- Cholesterol: 1131.5
- Sodium: 4440.2

27. Chef Joey's Dairy Free Pound Cake

Serving: 12-14 serving(s) | Prep: 25mins | Ready in:

Ingredients

- 3 cups white spelt flour (or cake flour)
- 1/2 teaspoon baking powder
- 1/4 teaspoon salt
- 1 cup Earth Balance margarine
- 2 1/2 cups raw sugar (sifted)
- 1 1/2 cups egg substitute (I used Nulaid Reddi Liquid Egg-its fat and cholesterol free)
- 1/4 cup lemon juice (about 2 lemons plus the zest from both lemons)
- 1 cup vegan sour cream

Direction

- Zest the lemons and set aside. Do this before juicing as it's easier.
- Set oven to 325'F.
- Grease a 16 cup tube pan. Dust with flour by swirling it around the bottom and sides. Then flour the tube as well. Tap out the excess.
- Sift the spelt, baking powder and salt together in a medium bowl and set aside.
- In the bowl of a stand mixer cream the margarine until it's light and fluffy.
- Add in the sifted sugar and beat for about 5 minutes making sure the sugar is well incorporated.
- Add the egg replacer in 1/4 cup increments until all added and make sure this is well mixed.
- Beat in the lemon zest and juice.
- With a good rubber spatula add in the sifted dry ingredients until well mixed.
- Mix in the vegan sour cream.
- Put the batter into your prepared tube cake pan.
- Bake for about 1 1/2 hours. Using a wooden kabob skewer test for done-ness. I stuck the skewer a few times near the middle as this is the thickest part. If it comes out clean then the cake is done.

- Cool on a metal rack for 15-20 minutes. Then run a knife around the outside of the cake.
- Turn the cake onto the metal cooling rack and then put it right side up. Let the cake cool completely.
- You can make this a few days ahead.
- Wrap in tin foil and store in the fridge.
- Remove what you're going to eat before serving and let come to room temperature.
- Bon Appetit!

Nutrition Information

- Calories: 176.9
- Sugar: 42.3
- Total Carbohydrate: 42.7
- Cholesterol: 0
- Sodium: 123.7
- Saturated Fat: 0
- Fiber: 0
- Protein: 3
- Total Fat: 0

28. Cherry Loaf "Pound Cake"

Serving: 1 Loaf, 15 serving(s) | Prep: 15mins | Ready in:

Ingredients

- 1 cup butter
- 1 cup berry sugar
- 3 eggs
- 2 cups flour
- 1/2 teaspoon salt
- 2 cups maraschino cherries

Direction

- Cream butter with sugar, beat until fluffy.
- Add eggs one at a time, beat after each addition.
- Mix flour and salt.
- Add flour mix to creamed mixture and blend thoroughly.

- Fold in cherries.
- Bake at 300 degrees for 1 hr. and 20 minute.

Nutrition Information

- Calories: 183.5
- Total Fat: 13.4
- Fiber: 0.5
- Sugar: 0.1
- Protein: 3.1
- Cholesterol: 69.7
- Saturated Fat: 8.1
- Sodium: 200.1
- Total Carbohydrate: 12.8

29. Chicken Noodle Pistachio Pound Cake

Serving: 1 cake, 10-12 serving(s) | Prep: 30mins | Ready in:

Ingredients

- 5 cups Bisquick
- 1 (3 1/2 ounce) box Jell-O instant pistachio pudding mix
- 1 teaspoon cinnamon
- 110 1/2 ounces Campbell's chicken noodle soup
- 1/2 cup brown sugar
- 1 (10 ounce) packageof thawed Green Giant frozen spinach
- 1 teaspoon yeast

Direction

- Preheat oven to 425 degrees.
- Note: Must use a mixer or an electric drill with a wide blade attachment.
- Pound Cake: Combine the spinach, yeast, brown sugar, and Bisquick with the mixer set on "Low" in a large bowl.
- Gently spoon the noodles and chicken into the batter. Be careful not to break the noodles!
- Pour the mixture into a bread pan and sprinkle cinnamon on top. Cover the pan with a damp towel and let the batter rise approximately 20 minutes.
- Place the pan into the preheated oven and bake until golden brownish-green.
- Icing: Strain the broth from the chicken noodle soup into a container and mix in the Jello Instant Pistachio Pudding. Stir until creamy. Chill for 45 minutes.
- Pour the icing over the cake as it cools. Serve with small cups of tomato juice.
- NOTE: Prep time includes 20 minute rising time.

Nutrition Information

- Calories: 300
- Saturated Fat: 2.4
- Sodium: 770.1
- Protein: 5
- Total Fat: 9.3
- Fiber: 1.5
- Sugar: 17.6
- Total Carbohydrate: 49
- Cholesterol: 1.2

30. Chocolate Almond Pound Cake

Serving: 2 loaves | Prep: 10mins | Ready in:

Ingredients

- FOR THE CAKE
- 1 1/2 cups chopped almonds, divided
- 1 (18 1/4 ounce) box devil's food cake mix
- 1 (3 1/2 ounce) box instant chocolate pudding mix
- 1 cup sour cream
- 4 large eggs
- 1/2 cup vegetable oil
- 2 teaspoons vanilla extract
- 1 cup miniature semisweet chocolate chips
- FOR THE GLAZE

- 1/2 cup powdered sugar
- 2 -3 teaspoons milk

Direction

- Coat two (9x5x3 inch) loaf pans with shortening and dust with unsweetened cocoa powder, tapping out excess.
- Place 1 cup of the almonds in a single layer on a baking sheet and toast in a preheated 350 degree oven for 7-8 minutes, stirring once or twice, until golden brown.
- Cool.
- FOR THE CAKE:
- In a large bowl, combine cake mix, pudding mix, sour cream, eggs, oil and vanilla and beat on medium speed with electric mixer for 4 minutes.
- Add mini chocolate chips and the 1 cup of toasted almonds and stir well.
- Pour batter into prepared pans; sprinkle remaining 1/2 cup of untoasted almonds on the top.
- Bake for 45-50 minutes or until cake tester inserted near center comes out clean.
- Place pans on wire racks and let cool for 15 minutes before turning cakes out to cool completely.
- FOR GLAZE:
- In a small bowl, combine powdered sugar and 2 teaspoons of milk, stirring until smooth.
- Add remaining teaspoons of milk if necessary to achieve desired consistency.
- Drizzle over cooled cakes.

Nutrition Information

- Calories: 3333.2
- Total Fat: 210.7
- Sodium: 3406.8
- Protein: 59.3
- Saturated Fat: 53.6
- Fiber: 25.3
- Sugar: 207.7
- Total Carbohydrate: 343.2
- Cholesterol: 474.3

31. Chocolate Chip Cream Cheese Pound Cake

Serving: 2 loaves | Prep: 15mins | Ready in:

Ingredients

- 3 cups flour
- 1/4 teaspoon salt
- 1 1/2 cups unsalted butter, at room temperature
- 8 ounces cream cheese, softened
- 3 cups sugar
- 6 eggs
- 1 1/2 teaspoons vanilla
- 1 1/2 cups semi-sweet chocolate chips

Direction

- In medium bowl, combine flour and salt.
- In large bowl, cream together butter, cream cheese and sugar. Add eggs one at a time.
- Add flour and vanilla. Stir in chocolate chips.
- Spread into prepared pans. Bake 90 minutes or until done.

Nutrition Information

- Calories: 4281.1
- Cholesterol: 1049
- Total Fat: 230.9
- Saturated Fat: 136.7
- Fiber: 12.5
- Protein: 51.7
- Sodium: 908
- Sugar: 373.3
- Total Carbohydrate: 529.7

32. Chocolate Chip Peanut Butter Pound Cake

Serving: 1 cake, 8-10 serving(s) | Prep: 15mins | Ready in:

Ingredients

- Cake ingredients
- 3 cups flour
- 1 teaspoon baking powder
- 1/2 teaspoon salt
- 1 cup peanut butter
- 1/2 cup butter
- 3 cups white sugar
- 6 eggs
- 2 teaspoons vanilla
- 1 1/2 cups chocolate chips
- Glaze ingredients
- 1 1/2 cups powdered sugar
- 1/4 cup milk
- 1/4 cup peanut butter
- 1/2 teaspoon vanilla
- 1/4 cup mini chocolate chip

Direction

- Preheat oven to 350 degrees.
- Stir together all cake ingredients, gently stirring in the chocolate chips last.
- Pour batter into pan.
- Bake for 1 hour and 20 minutes.
- Let cool for 20 minutes.
- Drizzle glaze over cake, then sprinkle mini chocolate chips on top.

Nutrition Information

- Calories: 1126.9
- Cholesterol: 171.1
- Protein: 21.6
- Saturated Fat: 19.5
- Sodium: 540.4
- Fiber: 5.9
- Sugar: 121.1
- Total Carbohydrate: 165.6

- Total Fat: 47.2

33. Chocolate Cream Cheese Pound Cake

Serving: 16 serving(s) | Prep: 15mins | Ready in:

Ingredients

- 1 (18 1/4 ounce) boxplain butter recipe fudge cake mix
- 1 (8 ounce) package cream cheese, at room temperature
- 1/2 cup water
- 1/2 cup vegetable oil
- 1/4 cup sugar
- 4 large eggs
- 2 teaspoons pure vanilla extract

Direction

- Place a rack in the center of the oven and preheat it to 325°F Lightly mist a 10-inch tube pan with vegetable oil spray, then dust with flour.
- Place the cake mix, cream cheese, water, oil, sugar, eggs and vanilla in a large mixing bowl.
- Blend on low speed for 1 minute.
- Stop the machine and scrape down the sides.
- Beat 2 minutes more on medium speed.
- The batter should look well-combined.
- Pour in the pan and bake 58 to 62 minutes or until the cake springs back when lightly pressed and is just starting to pull away from the sides.
- Remove cake to wire rack and allow it to cool for 20 minutes.
- Run a long sharp knife around the edge and invert it onto a rack.
- Then invert it onto another rack so the large side is up.
- Makes 16 servings.

Nutrition Information

- Calories: 280.1
- Saturated Fat: 5.4
- Sugar: 15.7
- Protein: 4.5
- Total Fat: 18
- Sodium: 326.4
- Fiber: 0.8
- Total Carbohydrate: 27.3
- Cholesterol: 68.5

34. Chocolate Hazelnut Orange Pound Cake

Serving: 12-15 serving(s) | Prep: 35mins | Ready in:

Ingredients

- 2 cups butter, at room temperature
- 2 1/2 cups sugar
- 6 eggs, lightly beaten
- 2 teaspoons vanilla extract
- 1 grated orange, rind of
- 4 cups unbleached white flour
- 2 teaspoons baking powder
- 1/2 cup orange juice
- 1/2 cup milk
- 1 cup ground toasted hazelnuts
- 1 cup coarsely chopped semisweet chocolate

Direction

- Preheat the oven to 350°F. Lightly butter a 10-inch Bundt pan and dust it with flour.
- In a large bowl, cream the butter and sugar until fluffy. Thoroughly beat in the eggs, vanilla, and orange peel.
- In a separate bowl, combine the flour and baking powder. Add the flour mixture by thirds, alternating first with the orange juice and then with the milk, and beat well after each addition. Stir in the nuts and chocolate by hand.

- Pour the batter into the prepared pan and bake for 1 1/4 to 1 1/2 hours, until a knife inserted in the center comes out clean.
- Cool the cake in the pan for 10 minutes; then turn it out and transfer to a wire rack to cool completely.

Nutrition Information

- Calories: 760.3
- Cholesterol: 188.5
- Protein: 11.3
- Fiber: 4.1
- Sugar: 43.5
- Total Carbohydrate: 80.7
- Total Fat: 46.6
- Saturated Fat: 24.6
- Sodium: 322.1

35. Chocolate Hazelnut Pound Cake With Shiny Chocolate Glaze

Serving: 16-20 serving(s) | Prep: 30mins | Ready in:

Ingredients

- 1 1/2 cups hazelnuts, about 6 to 7 ounces
- 8 ounces semisweet chocolate, cut into 1/4-inch pieces
- 16 tablespoons unsalted butter
- 1 cup sugar, divided
- 8 eggs, separated
- 1 cup all-purpose flour
- 1/4 teaspoon salt
- Glaze
- 1/3 cup water
- 1/3 cup light corn syrup
- 1 cup sugar
- 8 ounces semisweet chocolate, cut into 1/4-inch pieces

Direction

- Set a rack in the middle level of the oven and preheat to 350 degrees. Butter a 12-cup Bundt pan and flour the buttered surface.
- Shaking out the excess. Place hazelnuts in the bowl of a food processor fitted with the steel blade and pulse continuously until finely ground.
- Bring a small pan of water to a boil and remove from heat. Place chocolate in a heatproof bowl and set over the pan of water, stirring occasionally, until melted. Remove bowl from pan and set aside.
- In a large mixer bowl beat the butter and 1/2 cup of the sugar until soft and light. Beat in the chocolate and scrape bowl and beater(s).
- Beat in the egg yolks, one at a time. Scrape bowl and beater(s). Stir in the ground hazelnuts and the flour by hand.
- In a clean, dry mixer bowl, whip the egg whites with the salt on medium speed, until they are frothy. Continue whipping the egg whites until they are white and opaque, and beginning to hold their shape when the beater(s) are lifted. Increase the speed and gradually whip in the remaining 1/2 cup sugar, continuing to whip the egg whites until they hold a soft, glossy peak.
- Stir a quarter of the egg whites into the batter to lighten it, then fold in the remaining egg whites with a rubber spatula, and continue to fold until no streaks of egg white remain. Scrape the batter into the prepared pan.
- Bake the cake about 35 to 45 minutes, until it is well risen and a toothpick or skewer inserted between the edge of the pan and the central tube emerges clean. Place a rack on the pan and invert cake and pan to rack to cool. Remove pan after 5 minutes and allow cake to cool.
- For glaze, combine water, corn syrup and sugar in a saucepan and stir well to mix. Place over low heat and bring to a boil, stirring occasionally to dissolve sugar. Remove from heat and add chocolate.
- Swirl pan so that chocolate is submerged in hot syrup, then allow to stand 2 minutes. Whisk glaze smooth.
- Before glazing cake, cut a disk that will fit under the cake from stiff corrugated cardboard. Cut a hole in the canter corresponding to the central tube in the cake pan. Slide the cardboard under the cake and place it on a rack over a jelly roll pan. Pour glaze from pan onto highest point of cake, all around, allowing glaze to drip down outside and center of cake. Let glaze dry before moving cake.

Nutrition Information

- Calories: 505.4
- Saturated Fat: 17.8
- Sodium: 84.4
- Total Carbohydrate: 47.2
- Cholesterol: 136.3
- Protein: 9.6
- Total Fat: 36.6
- Fiber: 6.1
- Sugar: 27.9

36. Chocolate Orange Cream Cheese Pound Cake

Serving: 16 serving(s) | Prep: 15mins | Ready in:

Ingredients

- 1 (18 ounce) box chocolate cake mix
- 8 ounces cream cheese, softened
- 3/4 cup fresh orange juice
- 1/2 cup oil
- 1/4 cup sugar
- 4 eggs
- 2 teaspoons vanilla
- 1 teaspoon orange zest

Direction

- Preheat oven to 325. Grease and flour 12 cup Bundt or tube cake pan.

- Place all ingredients in mixing bowl, and mix at low speed for about 1 minute, scraping bowl constantly.
- Increase mixer speed to medium and beat for 2 minutes more, or until batter is well mixed.
- Pour into pans and bake for 60-65 minutes, or until tests done.
- Cool in pan for about 25 minutes, then remove from pan and cool completely before drizzling with a glaze made from powdered sugar and orange juice.

Nutrition Information

- Calories: 283.5
- Total Carbohydrate: 28.2
- Cholesterol: 68.5
- Saturated Fat: 5.4
- Sodium: 322.8
- Sugar: 16.5
- Protein: 4.6
- Total Fat: 18
- Fiber: 0.8

37. Chocolate Orange Sour Cream Pound Cake

Serving: 10-12 serving(s) | Prep: 25mins | Ready in:

Ingredients

- 1/4 cup semisweet chocolate, melted and cooled (optional)
- 3/4 cup unsalted butter
- 1 1/3 cups sugar
- 3 eggs
- 1 cup sour cream
- 2 teaspoons pure vanilla extract
- 1 1/2 teaspoons orange oil
- 1 orange, zest of, finely minced (optional)
- 1/4 cup milk
- 3/8 teaspoon salt
- 1/2 teaspoon baking soda
- 2 1/2 teaspoons baking powder
- 3 cups all-purpose flour
- 175 g terrys orange-shaped chocolate, minced or 1/2 cup miniature milk chocolate chips
- Garnish
- confectioners' sugar
- variety of melted chocolate
- Glaze
- orange juice
- confectioners' sugar

Direction

- Preheat the oven to 350°F
- Generously grease a 9 inch tube pan or Bundt cake pan or two 8 by 4 inch, or two 9 by 5 inch loaf pans with nonstick cooking spray.
- Melt the chocolate and set aside.
- Cream the butter and the sugar until fluffy.
- Beat in the eggs, sour cream, orange zest and extracts, blending well.
- Fold in the dry ingredients, scraping the bottom of the bowl to make sure it is all blended.
- Stir in the milk, and then fold in the chocolate.
- Remove 1/2 up of the batter and mix with the melted chocolate.
- Spoon white batter into pan and then drop spoonfuls of the chocolate batter on top of that. Swirl briefly with a knife to marbleize.
- Bake until cake springs back when lightly touched with fingertips, about 45-65 minutes (depending on pans used).
- Dust with confectioners' sugar or drizzle on melted white and dark chocolate or melted milk chocolate.
- Alternatively, you can glaze with an orange juice and confectioner's sugar glaze.

Nutrition Information

- Calories: 522.2
- Fiber: 3.9
- Sugar: 27.8
- Total Carbohydrate: 61.9
- Saturated Fat: 17.7

- Sodium: 290.8
- Cholesterol: 105.2
- Protein: 8.8
- Total Fat: 29.5

38. Chocolate Pound Cake With Fudge Icing

Serving: 12-16 serving(s) | Prep: 30mins | Ready in:

Ingredients

- Cake
- 1 cup unsalted butter
- 1/2 cup butter flavor shortening
- 3 cups granulated sugar
- 5 large eggs
- 3 cups all-purpose flour
- 1/2 cup unsweetened natural cocoa powder
- 2/3 teaspoon baking powder
- 1/4 teaspoon salt
- 1 teaspoon vanilla extract
- 1 1/4 cups whole milk
- Fudge Icing
- 2 cups granulated sugar
- 2/3 cup whole milk
- 1/2 cup unsalted butter
- 1/4 cup unsweetened natural cocoa powder
- 1/4 teaspoon salt
- 1 teaspoon vanilla extract

Direction

- Preheat oven to 325 degrees.
- Grease and flour a 12-cup tube pan; set aside.
- In large bowl, beat butter, shortening, and sugar at medium speed with an electric mixer until very creamy.
- Add eggs, one at a time, beating well after each addition.
- In another bowl, sift together flour, cocoa, baking powder, and salt.
- Add flour mixture to butter mixture, alternately with milk, beginning and ending with flour mixture.
- Pour batter into prepared pan.
- Bake for 1 hour 10 minutes, or until a wooden pick inserted in the center of cake comes out clean.
- Note: You may have to bake your cake longer than the stated time, depending on your oven.
- Let cool in pan for 15 minutes.
- Invert onto a cooling rack and let cool completely.
- Place cake on a cake plate, ready to frost, before making fudge icing.
- Frost with fudge icing as soon as it reaches the proper spreading consistency.
- For the icing, in saucepan, combine sugar, milk, butter, cocoa and salt.
- Bring to a boil over medium heat.
- Let boil for 2 minutes.
- Remove from heat and add vanilla.
- Beat at high speed with an electric mixer for 6-8 minutes, or until frosting becomes creamy and reaches a spreadable consistency.
- If making icing on a rainy day, it may take longer to reach a spreadable consistency.
- If you overbeat icing, or it begins to harden, add a little hot water, 1 teaspoon at a time, until icing is spreadable again.

Nutrition Information

- Calories: 783.2
- Total Fat: 35.9
- Sodium: 169.2
- Cholesterol: 142.4
- Saturated Fat: 18.6
- Fiber: 2.6
- Sugar: 85.5
- Total Carbohydrate: 112.5
- Protein: 8.4

39. Chocolate Pound Cake(Cook's Country)

Serving: 1 Loaf, 8 serving(s) | Prep: 20mins | Ready in:

Ingredients

- 1 cup all-purpose flour (5 ounces)
- 1 teaspoon salt
- 1/3 cup water, boiling
- 3/4 cup Dutch-processed cocoa powder (2 1/4 ounces)
- 2 ounces milk chocolate, chopped fine
- 16 tablespoons unsalted butter, softened
- 1 cup granulated sugar (7 ounces)
- 1/4 cup packed light brown sugar (1 3/4 ounces)
- 2 teaspoons vanilla extract
- 5 large eggs, room temperature

Direction

- 1. Adjust oven rack to lower-middle position and heat oven to 325 degrees. Grease and flour 8½ by 4½-inch loaf pan. Combine flour and salt in bowl. Pour water over cocoa and chocolate in second bowl and stir until chocolate is melted and no dry streaks of cocoa remain. Let mixture cool 5 minutes.
- 2. Using stand mixer fitted with paddle, beat butter, cocoa-chocolate mixture, granulated sugar, brown sugar, and vanilla on medium-high speed until fluffy, 2 to 3 minutes. Add eggs, one at a time, and beat until combined. Reduce speed to low and add flour mixture in 3 additions, scraping down bowl as needed, until just combined. Give batter final stir by hand (it may look curdled).
- 3. Scrape batter into prepared pan and gently tap pan on counter to release air bubbles. Bake until toothpick inserted in center comes out clean, 60 to 70 minutes. Cool cake in pan on wire rack for 10 minutes. Remove cake from pan and cool for 2 hours. Serve.

Nutrition Information

- Calories: 487.4
- Total Fat: 29.4
- Saturated Fat: 17.6
- Sodium: 348.4
- Fiber: 3.3
- Sugar: 35.7
- Total Carbohydrate: 52.9
- Cholesterol: 178.9
- Protein: 7.9

40. Chocolate Swirl Marble Pound Cake

Serving: 12 serving(s) | Prep: 40mins | Ready in:

Ingredients

- 2 cups sugar
- 1 cup butter, softened
- 3 1/2 cups flour
- 1 cup milk
- 1 1/2 teaspoons baking powder
- 2 teaspoons vanilla extract
- 1/4 teaspoon salt
- 4 eggs
- 1/4 cup unsweetened cocoa powder

Direction

- Heat oven to 350°F Grease a 10" tube pan.
- Beat sugar and butter until blended; then increase speed to high and beat until light and fluffy.
- Add flour and remaining ingredients EXCEPT cocoa. Beat at low speed until well mixed, scraping bowl often; then increase to high and beat 4 minutes longer, scraping bowl as needed.
- Scoop out 2 1/2 cups of batter into a small bowl. Whisk in cocoa powder.
- Alternately spoon vanilla and chocolate batters into prepared tube pan. Using a knife, cut and twist through batter to create a marble effect.

- Bake 60 minutes or until a toothpick comes out clean.
- Cool in pan on a wire rack for 10 minutes. Then run a spatula or knife around the pan to loosen the cake. Remove cake and cook on a wire rack.

Nutrition Information

- Calories: 441.3
- Saturated Fat: 10.9
- Fiber: 1.6
- Cholesterol: 114
- Protein: 7
- Total Fat: 18.4
- Sodium: 237.3
- Sugar: 33.7
- Total Carbohydrate: 63.4

41. Cindy's Coconut Pound Cake

Serving: 1 cake | Prep: 20mins | Ready in:

Ingredients

- 5 eggs
- 2 cups sugar
- 1 cup canola oil
- 2 cups flour, sifted
- 1 1/2 teaspoons baking powder
- 1/2 teaspoon salt
- 1/2 cup milk
- 1 teaspoon vanilla
- 1 cup coconut
- 1 teaspoon coconut extract
- SAUCE
- 1 cup sugar
- 1/2 cup water
- 1/4 cup butter
- 1 teaspoon coconut extract

Direction

- Grease and flour a tube pan. (Don't miss and spots or you won't get the cake out without breaking it.
- Beat 5 eggs.
- Add 2 cups sugar and beat well.
- Add 1 cup canola oil.
- Sift 2 cups flour, 1 1/2 tsp baking powder, 1/2 tsp salt. Add to egg mixture and blend well.
- Add to above mixture 1 cup coconut, 1/2 cup milk, 1 tsp vanilla, 1 tsp coconut extract.
- Mix well and pour into pan.
- Bake at 350F for 55 to 60 minutes. Let cook while sauce is cooling.
- For the sauce mix well, boil 1 minute and pour slowly over cake. Let cool in pan.

Nutrition Information

- Calories: 6599.4
- Total Fat: 349.7
- Sugar: 607.2
- Total Carbohydrate: 820.7
- Saturated Fat: 104.9
- Sodium: 2571
- Fiber: 20.6
- Cholesterol: 1069.1
- Protein: 67.6

42. Cinnamon Pound Cake

Serving: 1 loaf, 6 serving(s) | Prep: 30mins | Ready in:

Ingredients

- Cake
- 3/4 cup unsalted butter, room temperature
- 1 cup sugar
- 1 1/2 teaspoons vanilla extract
- 1 teaspoon finely grated lemon zest
- 2 large eggs, room temperature
- 1 1/2 cups all-purpose flour
- 1 teaspoon ground cinnamon
- 1/4 teaspoon baking soda
- 1 teaspoon fine salt

- 1/2 cup full-fat sour cream
- Topping
- 2 tablespoons light brown sugar, packed
- 1 1/2 tablespoons all-purpose flour
- 1 teaspoon ground cinnamon
- 1 1/2 tablespoons unsalted butter, melted

Direction

- Cake.
- Preheat oven to 325 °F. Grease an 8 ½ by 4 ½ inch loaf pan and dust lightly with flour, tapping out excess.
- Beat butter and sugar until light and fluffy. Beat in vanilla and lemon zest and add eggs one at a time, beating well after each addition. In a separate bowl, sift flour, cinnamon, baking soda and salt. Add half of the flour to the butter mixture, blending gently to incorporate. Stir in sour cream, then blend in remaining flour. Scrape batter into prepared pan.
- Topping.
- For topping, combine all ingredients to blend and sprinkle on top of cake. Bake for 55 to 65 minutes, until a tester inserted of the canter of the cake comes out clean. Allow to cool for 20 minutes before turning out to cool completely.

Nutrition Information

- Calories: 566.5
- Total Fat: 31.9
- Saturated Fat: 19.5
- Cholesterol: 147.6
- Protein: 6.4
- Sodium: 479.8
- Fiber: 1.3
- Sugar: 38.2
- Total Carbohydrate: 64.8

43. Cinnamon Swirled Almond Pound Cake

Serving: 12 serving(s) | Prep: 45mins | Ready in:

Ingredients

- 1 cup sliced almonds
- 1 tablespoon ground cinnamon
- 3 tablespoons almond paste
- 1 (18 1/4 ounce) package white cake mix
- 1 (3 1/2 ounce) package vanilla instant pudding mix
- 1 (8 ounce) container sour cream
- 4 eggs, lightly beaten
- 1/2 cup vegetable oil
- 1/2 cup Amaretto
- 1/2 cup water

Direction

- Preheat oven to 350 degrees.
- Grease and flour a 10-inch tube pan and set aside.
- Place the almond and cinnamon in the bowl of a food processor; process until finely chopped.
- Place one-third of the almond mixture in the bottom of the prepared pan.
- Add the almond paste to the remaining almond mixture and stir until well combined.
- In the bowl of an electric mixer, combine the cake mix, pudding mix, sour cream, eggs, oil, amaretto, and water.
- Beat on low speed to combine and then increase to medium speed and beat 2 minutes.
- Spoon one-third of the batter into the prepared pan.
- Evenly sprinkle half the almond paste mixture over the batter.
- Repeat and end with the last of the batter on top.
- Bake 55 minutes, or until a tester inserted in the center comes out clean.
- Cool in the pan 10 minutes and then cool completely on a wire rack before serving.

Nutrition Information

- Calories: 419.9
- Sugar: 33.5
- Saturated Fat: 5.1
- Fiber: 1.8
- Sodium: 444.5
- Total Carbohydrate: 45.9
- Cholesterol: 72.4
- Protein: 6.4
- Total Fat: 24.2

44. Citrus Pound Cake With Lemon Cream Cheese Frosting

Serving: 1 cake | Prep: 18mins | Ready in:

Ingredients

- CAKE
- 6 large eggs, room temperature
- 1 cup unsalted butter, room temperature
- 3 cups pure cane granulated sugar
- 1 tablespoon lemon flavoring (Lemon, LorAnn Gourmet baking emulsion)
- 1 lemon, zested
- 2 1/2 teaspoons fresh lemon juice
- 3 cups cake flour
- 1 cup heavy whipping cream
- LEMON CREAM CHEESE FROSTING
- 8 ounces cream cheese, softened
- 4 tablespoons unsalted butter, room temperature
- 3 1/2 teaspoons fresh lemon juice
- 1 lemon, zested
- 4 cups powdered sugar
- heavy whipping cream

Direction

- For cake: Preheat oven to 350 F, and prepare pans with parchment circles and lightly spray with baking spray. Using a stand mixer or hand mixer, cream butter and sugar until light and fluffy, approximately 3 minutes. Add baking emulsion, lemon zest, lemon juice and mix well. Add eggs one at a time and mix until well incorporated. Add flour and heavy whipping cream, alternating each a third at a time, ending with the whipping cream. Mix until combines, but do not over mix, approximately 2 minutes.
- Divide batter between pans. Bake in preheated oven for 38 to 40 minutes. Check cake at 38 minutes to make sure it is not over baking (cake will pull away from the edges). Insert a cake tester or toothpick at the center of the cake. If toothpick removes clean, then it is done. Place on cooling racks in pan for 15 minutes. Remove from pan and let cake cool completely.
- For the frosting: In a large bowl, cream together cream cheese and butter until smooth and fluffy. Add lemon juice, zest, and powdered sugar and stir to combine. Add whipping cream 1 or 2 tablespoons at a time to reach spreadable consistency. Use immediately. Yields 3 cups.

Nutrition Information

- Calories: 9779.1
- Saturated Fat: 254.4
- Sodium: 1303.4
- Fiber: 10.3
- Total Fat: 428.5
- Sugar: 1082
- Total Carbohydrate: 1430.5
- Cholesterol: 2302.2
- Protein: 93.5

45. Clara's Pound Cake

Serving: 16 serving(s) | Prep: 15mins | Ready in:

Ingredients

- 1/2 cup butter
- 1/2 cup Crisco

- 3 cups sugar
- 5 eggs
- 3 cups all-purpose flour
- 1 teaspoon baking powder
- 1 pinch salt
- 1 cup milk
- 2 teaspoons vanilla
- Crisco or butter
- powdered sugar

Direction

- Grease a 10" tube pan with Crisco or butter and, instead of using flour to dust the pan, use powdered sugar to coat the greased pan. Set aside.
- Cream together butter and Crisco.
- Add sugar and mix well.
- Add eggs one at time.
- Sift dry ingredients.
- Add alternately with milk and vanilla.
- Pour into prepared 10" tube pan.
- Bake at 300 degrees F for one hour.
- Turn oven up to 325 degrees F and bake for 15 additional minutes.

Nutrition Information

- Calories: 372.3
- Protein: 5
- Total Fat: 14.5
- Sugar: 37.7
- Total Carbohydrate: 56.4
- Cholesterol: 83.5
- Saturated Fat: 6.5
- Sodium: 103.1
- Fiber: 0.6

46. Cloverbloom Pound Cake

Serving: 10 serving(s) | Prep: 10mins | Ready in:

Ingredients

- 1 cup butter, softened
- 1 1/4 cups sugar
- 5 eggs
- 2 1/4 cups flour
- 1/2 teaspoon baking powder
- 1/4 teaspoon salt
- 1 teaspoon vanilla

Direction

- Cream butter until fluffy.
- Add sugar gradually and continue to cream after each addition.
- Add egg yolks which have been beaten until thick and lemon colored.
- Beat egg whites until stiff but not dry and fold into batter.
- Fold in flour, powder and salt sifted together.
- Add vanilla and pour into a loaf pan which has been lined with oiled paper.
- Bake at 325* for 1 1/4- 1 1/2 hours.

Nutrition Information

- Calories: 400
- Fiber: 0.8
- Total Carbohydrate: 46.8
- Cholesterol: 154.6
- Saturated Fat: 12.5
- Sodium: 242.6
- Total Fat: 21.2
- Sugar: 25.3
- Protein: 6.2

47. Coconut Oil Pound Cake With Almonds And Lime Zest

Serving: 8-10 serving(s) | Prep: 10mins | Ready in:

Ingredients

- 1/2 cup almonds, sliced
- 1 cup sugar
- 2 tablespoons sugar

- 1/2 cup organic virgin coconut oil
- 3/4 cup milk
- 3 large eggs
- lime zest (1 lime)
- 1 3/4 cups all-purpose flour
- 1 3/4 teaspoons baking powder
- 1/4 teaspoon nutmeg, freshly grated
- 1/4 teaspoon kosher salt

Direction

- Preheat oven to 350 degrees F; grease a 9x5 inch loaf pan.
- Prepare the topping in a small bowl by combining the almonds, 2 tablespoons sugar, and 1 tablespoon water; set aside.
- Next, melt the coconut oil in a small pan, then pour it into a large bowl; whisk in the remaining sugar, milk, eggs, and lime zest.
- Then in a medium bowl, whisk together the dry ingredients: flour, baking powder, nutmeg, and salt; fold the dry ingredients into the wet ingredients until combined.
- Pour the batter into the loaf pan and smooth out with a spatula; sprinkle the almond topping on top.
- Bake until golden and a toothpick inserted in the center comes out clean, about 60 minutes; allow to cool on a wire rack 10 minutes before attempting to remove from the loaf pan.
- Cool completely before serving.

Nutrition Information

- Calories: 302.1
- Protein: 7.8
- Saturated Fat: 1.5
- Sodium: 201.8
- Fiber: 1.7
- Sugar: 28.7
- Total Carbohydrate: 52.3
- Total Fat: 7.4
- Cholesterol: 73

48. Copycat Starbucks Raspberry Swirl Pound Cake

Serving: 1 9x5-inch loaf pan, 8 serving(s) | Prep: 10mins | Ready in:

Ingredients

- POUND CAKE
- 1 (18 ounce) box poundcake mix
- 1/4 cup softened butter
- 2 eggs
- 2/3 cup milk
- 1 teaspoon lemon juice
- 1/3 cup seedless raspberry spreadable fruit
- 6 drops red food coloring (optional)
- ICING
- 8 ounces softened cream cheese
- 1 cup powdered sugar
- 1 teaspoon lemon juice

Direction

- Preheat oven to 350°F.
- Grease and flour 9x5-inch loaf pan.
- Combine cake mix, milk, eggs and butter and slowly beat until incorporated (30 seconds). Beat at medium and additional 2 minutes.
- Transfer about 1/3 of batter to another bowl.
- Add raspberry spread and food coloring to new bowl and stir to mix well.
- Add lemon juice to first bowl and mix well.
- Add a layer of white batter to pan. Add alternating layers of red and white.
- Bake 55-60 minutes.
- Allow to cool.
- Beat cream cheese on medium-high speed until light and fluffy (4-5 minutes).
- Add powdered sugar and mix until combined.
- Add lemon juice mixing on low until smooth.

Nutrition Information

- Calories: 237.5
- Protein: 4
- Total Fat: 17.4

- Saturated Fat: 10
- Fiber: 0
- Sugar: 15.7
- Total Carbohydrate: 17.2
- Sodium: 169.8
- Cholesterol: 95.8

- Sodium: 423.1
- Sugar: 58.1
- Total Carbohydrate: 87.3
- Cholesterol: 46.5
- Total Fat: 14.2
- Fiber: 3
- Protein: 6.1

49. Country Pound Cake From "Today In Mississippi."

Serving: 12 slices, 12 serving(s) | Prep: 30mins | Ready in:

Ingredients

- 1/3 cup vegetable oil
- 3 cups sugar
- 3 eggs, beaten
- 1 cup crushed pineapple, with juice
- 2 cups mashed bananas
- 1 cup chopped pecans
- 3 cups all-purpose flour
- 2 teaspoons baking soda
- 1 teaspoon salt
- 1 teaspoon cinnamon
- 1 1/2 teaspoons vanilla extract
- 1/4 teaspoon nutmeg (grated preferable)

Direction

- Mix vegetable oil, sugar, and eggs. Add pineapple, banana, and pecans.
- In a separate bowl, mix flour, baking soda, and salt.
- Add to sugar mixture. Add cinnamon, vanilla, and cherries.
- Grate nutmeg over mixture.
- Pour into a tube pan and bake at 525 to 350 degrees for 1 1/2 hours.

Nutrition Information

- Calories: 489.5
- Saturated Fat: 1.8

50. Cranberry Glazed Pound Cake

Serving: 16 serving(s) | Prep: 20mins | Ready in:

Ingredients

- Cake
- 2 cups butter, softened
- 3 cups sugar
- 12 egg yolks, well beaten
- 12 egg whites, beaten to stiff peaks
- 4 cups flour
- Cranberry Glaze
- 2 cups water
- 2 cups sugar
- 1 lb cranberries (4 cups)

Direction

- Cake: Cream butter and sugar.
- Alternately add egg yolks, egg whites and flour to butter mixture.
- Beat until light and smooth.
- Pour into greased and floured 10" tube pan.
- Bake in preheated 325* oven about 1 1/2 hours or until golden brown.
- Cool in pan 30 minutes before removing.
- Drizzle cooled Cranberry Glaze over cake.
- Decorate with whole cranberries, if desired.
- Cranberry Glaze: In a saucepan, bring water and sugar to rapid boil.
- Simmer 10 minutes and add cranberries.
- Cook until cranberries pop, about 5 minutes.
- Remove cranberries with slotted spoon and discard or save for another use.
- Continue to cook syrup until thickened, about 20 minutes.

- Allow to cool before using.

Nutrition Information

- Calories: 622
- Total Fat: 26.4
- Sodium: 211.8
- Sugar: 63.9
- Total Carbohydrate: 90.4
- Saturated Fat: 15.7
- Fiber: 2.1
- Cholesterol: 202.6
- Protein: 8.1

51. Cranberry Orange Pound Cake With Butter Rum Sauce

Serving: 16 serving(s) | Prep: 30mins | Ready in:

Ingredients

- Cake
- 2 3/4 cups sugar
- 1 1/2 cups butter or 1 1/2 cups margarine, softened
- 1 teaspoon vanilla
- 1 teaspoon orange zest
- 6 eggs
- 3 cups flour
- 1 teaspoon baking powder
- 1/2 teaspoon salt
- 1 (8 ounce) carton sour cream
- 1 1/2 cups chopped fresh cranberries or 1 1/2 cups frozen cranberries (do not thaw)
- Butter Rum Sauce
- 1 cup sugar
- 1 tablespoon flour
- 1/2 cup half-and-half
- 1/2 cup butter
- 4 teaspoons light rum or 1/4 teaspoon rum extract

Direction

- Heat oven to 350 degrees.
- Generously grease and lightly flour 12 cup fluted tube pan.
- In large bowl, beat 2 3/4 cups sugar and 1 1/2 cups butter until light and fluffy.
- Add vanilla and orange peel.
- Add eggs 1 at a time, beating well after each addition.
- In medium bowl, combine 3 cups flour, baking powder and salt.
- Add alternately with sour cream, beating well after each addition.
- Gently stir in cranberries.
- Pour batter into greased and floured pan.
- Bake at 350 degree for 65 to 75 minutes or until toothpick inserted in center comes out clean.
- Cool 15 minutes.
- Remove from pan.
- Meanwhile, in small saucepan combine 1 cup sugar and 1 Tbsp. flour.
- Stir in half-and-half and 1/2 cup butter.
- Cook over medium heat until thickened and bubbly, stirring constantly.
- Remove from heat; stir in rum.
- Serve warm sauce over cake.

Nutrition Information

- Calories: 545.4
- Sugar: 47.9
- Total Carbohydrate: 67.3
- Saturated Fat: 17.5
- Sodium: 340.8
- Fiber: 1.1
- Cholesterol: 141.3
- Protein: 5.6
- Total Fat: 28.9

52. Cream Cheese Pound Cake With Strawberries And Cream

Serving: 1 10inch cake | Prep: 10mins | Ready in:

Ingredients

- 1 (16 ounce) container fresh strawberries, sliced
- 2 tablespoons sugar
- 1 cup butter, softened
- 1 (8 ounce) package cream cheese, softened
- 2 1/2 cups sugar
- 6 large eggs
- 3 cups sifted cake flour
- 1/8 teaspoon salt
- 1 1/2 teaspoons vanilla extract
- 1 cup whipping cream
- 3 tablespoons sugar
- strawberry syrup (see recipe I posted Strawberry Sauce)
- 1 whole fresh strawberries, garnish

Direction

- Sprinkle sliced strawberries with 2 tablespoons sugar; cover and chill until ready to serve.
- Beat butter and cream cheese at medium speed with an electric mixer until creamy; gradually add 2 1/2 cups sugar, beating well.
- Add eggs, 1 at a time, beating until combined.
- Stir in flour by hand just until moistened.
- Stir in salt and vanilla.
- Pour batter into a greased and floured 10-inch tube pan.
- Bake at 300° for 1 hour and 50 minutes or until a wooden pick inserted in center comes out clean.
- Cool in pan on a wire rack 10 to 15 minutes; remove from pan, and let cool completely on wire rack.
- Cut into slices.
- Beat whipping cream and 3 tablespoons sugar at high speed with an electric mixer until stiff peaks form.
- Serve with cake; top with strawberry mixture, and drizzle with Strawberry Syrup.
- Garnish, if desired.
- Note: Great results for this recipe were gotten from using a hand mixer and then stirring the flour in by hand.

- High-powered stand mixers can over beat some pound cakes, giving them a tough texture.

Nutrition Information

- Calories: 7516.1
- Total Fat: 386
- Total Carbohydrate: 935.5
- Cholesterol: 2332.6
- Saturated Fat: 231.1
- Sodium: 2793.4
- Fiber: 16.4
- Sugar: 589.6
- Protein: 98.5

53. Cream Cheese And Nutella Filled Pound Cake

Serving: 1 loaf cake, 12 serving(s) | Prep: 10mins | Ready in:

Ingredients

- 1 butter pound cake, loaf pan type (store bought or homemade)
- 6 ounces cream cheese, softened
- 1/3 cup powdered sugar
- 1/2 cup toffee pieces, chopped fine (optional)
- 3/4 cup nutella (or chocolate icing)

Direction

- Cut pound cake in half horizontally (or in 3 even horizontal slices and make it even more fanciful. Just half the filling for each layer). Using an electric mixer, beat cream cheese and powdered sugar together until light and fluffy.
- Spread cream cheese on bottom piece of cake. Sprinkle with toffee bits (if using) and gently press the pieces into the cream cheese. Spread the other half of the pound cake with Nutella.
- Place Nutella cake over top of cream cheese side (like a sandwich). Immediately wrap cake

tightly in foil, place back into loaf pan, and refrigerate 2 hrs. Or overnight.
- When ready to serve, cut into 6 wide slices then cut the slices in half (making 12 pieces total).

Nutrition Information

- Calories: 259.5
- Saturated Fat: 7
- Sodium: 149.1
- Fiber: 1.1
- Cholesterol: 70.8
- Total Fat: 15.4
- Sugar: 13.4
- Total Carbohydrate: 27.4
- Protein: 3.5

54. Crusty Top, Sour Cream Pound Cake

Serving: 12 serving(s) | Prep: 20mins | Ready in:

Ingredients

- 1 cup oleo
- 3 cups sugar
- 6 eggs
- 1 cup sour cream
- 1/4 teaspoon baking soda
- 3 cups flour
- 1 teaspoon vanilla

Direction

- Sift flour and measure; resift twice with soda.
- Set aside.
- Cream oleo and add the sugar slowly, beating constantly to cream well.
- Add eggs, 1 at a time, beating after each addition.
- Stir in sour cream.
- Add flour mixture, 1/2 cup at a time, beating well.

- Stir in vanilla and turn batter into a well-greased and floured 10-inch tube pan.
- Bake in 325°F oven about 1 1/2 hours.
- Place pan on rack to cool 5 minutes.
- Loosen cake around edge of pan.
- Turn cake onto rack to cool completely.

Nutrition Information

- Calories: 381
- Total Carbohydrate: 74.6
- Protein: 6.8
- Total Fat: 6.5
- Sodium: 78.2
- Cholesterol: 103
- Saturated Fat: 3
- Fiber: 0.8
- Sugar: 50.8

55. Crystallized Ginger Yoghurt Pound Cake

Serving: 1 large Bundt Cake | Prep: 20mins | Ready in:

Ingredients

- 1 cup butter, at room temperature
- 1 1/2 cups sugar
- 2 teaspoons vanilla extract
- 1/2 teaspoon almond extract
- 4 eggs, at room temperature
- 2 1/2 cups all-purpose flour
- 2 1/2 teaspoons baking powder
- 1 teaspoon salt
- 1 1/2 cups Greek yogurt (sour cream can be used instead)
- 3/4 cup crystallized ginger, cut in tiny pieces

Direction

- Preheat oven to 300F (a low temperature, but it works); butter and flour a Bundt pan (mine is no-stick but I still butter and flour it).

- With mixer beat butter for a couple of minutes until white; add sugar and extracts and beat a few minutes longer (about 8-9 minutes in all); Add eggs, one at a time, beating after each addition; With mixer on low (to avoid getting flour dust all over the kitchen) add flour, baking powder and salt alternately with yoghurt; beat in ginger; this makes a very thick batter; Spoon into prepared Bundt pan and bake for 75 minutes (but start checking with toothpick to see if it's done after an hour (temperatures vary from oven to oven).
- Variations: I often use the 'base' recipe (omitting the ginger) and 'marble some of the batter with cocoa (add a tablespoonful or so of milk and 2 heaping tablespoonfuls of cocoa to 1/3 of the batter); or make a nut cake by stirring in 1 1/2 cups of the flour-dusted, toasted nuts of your choice (a sprinkle of freshly-grated nutmeg is great in this version); our current favorite is chocolate, chocolate/chip where I add 3 tablespoonfuls of cocoa to the batter (along with a couple of tablespoonfuls of milk - or buttermilk if you have it) and then stir in 1 1/2 cups of flour-dusted chocolate chips at the end, before spooning into pan.

Nutrition Information

- Calories: 4248.2
- Fiber: 8.5
- Sugar: 302.4
- Total Carbohydrate: 544.1
- Cholesterol: 1232
- Total Fat: 206.2
- Saturated Fat: 123.3
- Sodium: 5148.1
- Protein: 59.4

56. Daphne Oz's Coconut Pound Cake

Serving: 1 cake, 10 serving(s) | Prep: 15mins | Ready in:

Ingredients

- 4 eggs
- 2 cups sugar
- 1 cup unsalted butter
- 3 cups flour
- 1/2 teaspoon baking powder
- 1/2 salt
- 1 cup buttermilk
- 1 cup flaked coconut, unsweetened
- 1 cup pecans, chopped
- GLAZE
- 1/2 water
- 2 tablespoons salted butter
- 1 cup sugar
- powdered sugar, for dusting

Direction

- Preheat oven to 350 degrees Fahrenheit.
- In a large bowl, combine eggs, sugar and butter; beat with an electric mixer until light and fluffy, approximately 3 minutes.
- Combine flour, baking powder and salt in a separate bowl.
- Add flour mixture to batter alternately with buttermilk, in 3 parts; mix gently until just moistened.
- Stir in coconut and pecans.
- Pour batter into a pound cake mold (loaf shaped pan).
- Bake for 60 minutes or until a knife inserted in the center comes out clean.
- For the glaze:
- Five minutes before cake is finished baking make the glaze.
- Combine water, butter and sugar in a saucepan and bring to a boil. Reduce heat and cook for 5 minutes.
- Slowly pour half the syrup over the cake (bottom), invert onto a serving plate and pour remaining syrup over the top.

- Dust with powdered sugar.
- Let stand for 10 minutes and eat warm!

Nutrition Information

- Calories: 704.4
- Total Fat: 33.4
- Saturated Fat: 16.9
- Sugar: 64.8
- Total Carbohydrate: 95.9
- Sodium: 120.6
- Fiber: 2.9
- Cholesterol: 130.3
- Protein: 8.7

57. Devil's Food Pound Cake

Serving: 12 serving(s) | Prep: 15mins | Ready in:

Ingredients

- Cake
- 18 ounces devil's food cake mix
- 5 1/3 ounces instant chocolate pudding mix
- 4 eggs
- 1 1/2 cups water
- 1/2 cup vegetable oil
- Glaze
- 1 cup powdered sugar
- 1/2 teaspoon vanilla
- 2 tablespoons milk

Direction

- Preheat oven to 350*F.
- Cake--.
- Grease and flour Bundt pan.
- Combine cake ingredients and beat 2 minute on med. speed.
- Bake 50-60 min until toothpick comes out clean.
- Cool until comfortable to touch and invert onto serving plate.

- Allow to cool completely.
- Glaze--.
- Mix together glaze ingredients. If too dry, add a few drops of milk. If too runny, add a little powdered sugar.
- Drizzle glaze over cake.
- Enjoy!

Nutrition Information

- Calories: 375
- Total Carbohydrate: 52.2
- Total Fat: 17.7
- Sodium: 554.8
- Cholesterol: 70.9
- Protein: 5
- Saturated Fat: 3.2
- Fiber: 1.5
- Sugar: 32.7

58. Devil's Food Pound Cake With Chocolate Glaze

Serving: 16 serving(s) | Prep: 15mins | Ready in:

Ingredients

- 1 (18 1/4 ounce) package devil's food cake mix (Duncan Hines Moist Deluxe Devil's Food)
- 1 (3 1/2 ounce) package instant chocolate pudding mix
- 1/2 cup Crisco cooking oil
- 1 cup water
- 4 eggs
- 2 tablespoons cocoa
- 1 2/3 tablespoons water
- 1 tablespoon oil
- 1 tablespoon corn syrup
- 1 cup confectioners' sugar

Direction

- Preheat oven to 350 degrees.

- Blend all ingredients in a large bowl.
- Beat at medium speed for 2 minutes, careful not to overmix.
- Bake in a greased and floured 10-inch tube pan at 350 degrees for 50-60 minutes.
- Cake will be done when center springs back when touched lightly.
- Let cool right side up for 25 minutes.
- Remove from pan.
- To make the chocolate glaze, combine the cocoa, water oil and corn syrup in a small saucepan. Cook and stir over low heat until mixture is smooth. Remove from heat.
- Immediately beat in 1 cup confectioners' sugar.
- Drizzle over cake.

Nutrition Information

- Calories: 282.9
- Protein: 3.8
- Sodium: 373.2
- Cholesterol: 52.9
- Fiber: 1.1
- Sugar: 23.3
- Total Carbohydrate: 37.9
- Total Fat: 14.1
- Saturated Fat: 2.5

59. Double Peanut Butter Pound Cake

Serving: 1 cake, 16 serving(s) | Prep: 30mins | Ready in:

Ingredients

- 1 cup butter, softened
- 3/4 cup creamy peanut butter
- 3 cups sugar
- 2 teaspoons vanilla
- 5 eggs
- 3 cups flour
- 1/2 teaspoon baking powder
- 1/2 teaspoon salt
- 1 cup milk
- Frosting
- 1/2 cup peanut butter
- 1/2 cup corn syrup
- 2 cups powdered sugar
- 1 tablespoon milk
- 1 teaspoon vanilla

Direction

- Heat oven to 350. Grease and flour 10 inch tube pan.
- In large mixing bowl, combine butter, peanut butter, sugar, and vanilla; beat until light and fluffy. Add eggs, one at a time, beating well after each addition.
- In another bowl, combine flour, baking powder, and salt; stir into butter mixture alternately with milk. Pour into pan.
- Bake at 350 F until toothpick inserted in center comes out clean, about 1 hour and 15-30 minutes.
- Cool in pan 15 minutes on wire rack. Remove from pan. Cool completely on wire rack. Drizzle cake with Peanut Butter Frosting.
- Frosting (Sometimes I make only half of this as it makes a LOT):
- In sauce pan over low heat, melt 1/2 cup each of peanut butter and corn syrup. Stir in 2 cups powdered sugar, 1 T. milk, and 1 t. vanilla; mix until smooth.

Nutrition Information

- Calories: 571.3
- Total Fat: 24
- Fiber: 1.8
- Total Carbohydrate: 82.7
- Cholesterol: 90.9
- Saturated Fat: 10.3
- Sodium: 309.4
- Sugar: 56.7
- Protein: 10.1

60. Earl Grey Pound Cake With Lemon Curd

Serving: 12 mini cakes | Prep: 25mins | Ready in:

Ingredients

- 1 1/2 cups butter
- 6 eggs
- 1 1/2 cups sour cream
- 3 1/3 cups all-purpose flour
- 4 teaspoons finely ground earl grey tea, leaves*
- 1 1/2 teaspoons baking powder
- 1/2 teaspoon salt
- 1/4 teaspoon baking soda
- 1 1/2 cups granulated sugar
- 1 1/2 teaspoons vanilla
- 1 1/2 cups lemon curd (about one and a half 10-oz. jars)

Direction

- Let the butter, eggs, and sour cream stand at room temperature for 30 minutes.
- Preheat oven to 350 degrees F. Grease and flour 12 individual fluted tube pans; set aside.
- In a large bowl combine flour, ground tea leaves, baking powder, salt, and soda; set aside.
- In a very large mixing bowl beat butter with an electric mixer on medium-high speed for 1 to 2 minutes.
- Add granulated sugar; continue beating 5 minutes.
- Beat in the eggs, 1 at a time, scraping sides of bowl after each addition.
- Beat in vanilla (Mixture may appear curdled)
- Alternately add flour mixture and sour cream to butter mixture, beating on low speed after each addition until combined.
- Spoon batter into prepared pans, filling two-thirds full.
- Bake 25 minutes or until pick inserted near center comes out clean.
- Cool in pans on racks 10 minutes.
- Remove; cool on racks.
- TO FINISH:
- Split cakes in half. Place tops on plates upside down; spread with curd.
- Add bottoms to create a proper looking Bundt cake.
- Sprinkle powdered sugar.
- *TIP:
- For 4 teaspoons ground Earl Grey tea leaves, open bags with finely ground tea leaves (5 bags) or use mortar and pestle to finely grind loose Earl Grey tea leaves; measure 4 teaspoons.).

Nutrition Information

- Calories: 519.6
- Total Fat: 31.4
- Saturated Fat: 18.7
- Sodium: 430.6
- Fiber: 0.9
- Protein: 7.6
- Sugar: 26.2
- Total Carbohydrate: 52.7
- Cholesterol: 169

61. Early American Cornmeal Pound Cake

Serving: 1 cake | Prep: 10mins | Ready in:

Ingredients

- 6 tablespoons butter
- 1 cup sugar
- 4 eggs
- 1 1/4 cups sifted pastry flour
- 3/4 teaspoon baking powder
- 1/4 cup sifted white cornmeal
- 1/8 teaspoon freshly grated nutmeg (or 1/4 teaspoon prepared ground nutmeg)
- 1/4 teaspoon ground cinnamon

- 1/2 teaspoon vanilla
- 2 teaspoons brandy, preferably apple brandy

Direction

- Thoroughly cream butter and sugar until fluffy.
- Beat in the eggs, one at a time (an electric mixer may be used for these first two steps).
- Sift together the flour, baking powder, and cornmeal; combine spices with flour mixture.
- Blend by hand the dry ingredients into the batter alternately with the brandy and vanilla.
- Pour into a greased shallow cake pan, 8-inches square or 10-inches by 6-inches, the pan lined with wax paper.
- Bake at 325°F for 1 1/2 hours.
- Remove from oven and allow to cool for 10 minutes.
- Invert on a cake rack and strip of the wax paper.
- Serve and enjoy--and prepare to serve second helpings!

Nutrition Information

- Calories: 2447.9
- Total Fat: 91.7
- Saturated Fat: 50.4
- Sodium: 1057.6
- Fiber: 5.5
- Cholesterol: 1029.2
- Sugar: 202.5
- Total Carbohydrate: 360.3
- Protein: 42.5

62. Fannie Farmer's Pound Cake

Serving: 12 serving(s) | Prep: 15mins | Ready in:

Ingredients

- 1/2 lb butter
- 1 3/4 cups sugar

- 5 eggs
- 1 3/4 cups flour
- 1/2 teaspoon salt
- 2 teaspoons vanilla

Direction

- Preheat oven to 350 degrees.
- Cream butter and sugar with electric mixer.
- Beat eggs into mix.
- Stir in flour, salt, vanilla. Beat vigorously.
- Pour into greased and floured loaf pan.
- Bake at 350 degrees for 70-80 minutes.

Nutrition Information

- Calories: 347.5
- Cholesterol: 128.8
- Protein: 4.7
- Saturated Fat: 10.4
- Sodium: 235.4
- Fiber: 0.5
- Sugar: 29.4
- Total Carbohydrate: 43.3
- Total Fat: 17.6

63. Five Flavor Pound Cake

Serving: 1 Bundt cake, 12 serving(s) | Prep: 20mins | Ready in:

Ingredients

- Cake
- 1 cup butter, softened
- 1/2 cup shortening
- 3 cups granulated sugar
- 5 eggs, beaten
- 3 cups all-purpose flour
- 1/2 teaspoon baking powder
- 1 pinch salt
- 1 cup milk
- 1 teaspoon coconut extract
- 1 teaspoon lemon extract

- 1 teaspoon rum extract
- 1 teaspoon butter flavor extract
- 1 teaspoon vanilla extract
- Glaze
- 1/2 cup white sugar
- 1/4 cup water
- 1/2 teaspoon coconut extract
- 1/2 teaspoon rum extract
- 1/2 teaspoon butter flavor extract
- 1/2 teaspoon lemon extract
- 1/2 teaspoon vanilla extract

Direction

- Preheat oven to 325°F.
- Grease a 10-inch tube or Bundt cake pan.
- In small bowl, combine flour, baking powder and salt; set aside.
- In a measuring cup, combine the milk and 1 teaspoon of each of the 5 extracts; set aside.
- In mixing bowl, cream butter, shortening and 3 cups of sugar until light and fluffy.
- Add eggs one at a time and beat until smooth.
- Beat in flour mixture alternately with milk mixture, beginning and ending with flour mixture.
- Spoon mixture into prepared pan.
- Bake for 1 1/2 hours, or until cake tests done.
- Let cake cool for 5 minutes and then pour 1/2 of glaze over cake (while still in pan).
- Let sit for another 5 minutes and then turn cake out of pan onto wire rack (with waxed paper under rack to catch drippings).
- Slowly spoon remaining glaze onto top of hot cake.
- Cool completely before serving.
- To make the Five Flavor Glaze: In saucepan, combine 1/2 cup sugar, water and 1/2 teaspoon of each of the 5 extracts.
- Bring to a boil, stirring until sugar is dissolved.
- Variations: Six Flavor Cake/Glaze: Add 1 teaspoon of almond extract to Five Flavor Cake ingredients and 1/2 teaspoon almond extract to Five Flavor Glaze ingredients.
- Seven Flavor Cake/Glaze: Add 1 teaspoon pineapple flavored extract to Six Flavor Cake

and 1/2 teaspoon pineapple flavored extract to Six Flavor Glaze.

Nutrition Information

- Calories: 600.6
- Cholesterol: 121
- Total Fat: 26.9
- Sugar: 58.6
- Total Carbohydrate: 83.5
- Protein: 6.7
- Saturated Fat: 13
- Sodium: 204.2
- Fiber: 0.8

64. Four Flavor Pound Cake

Serving: 1 cake, 10-16 serving(s) | Prep: 20mins | Ready in:

Ingredients

- 1 cup butter
- 1/2 cup shortening
- 3 cups sugar
- 5 eggs (well beaten)
- 3 cups all-purpose flour
- 1/2 teaspoon baking powder
- 1 cup sweet milk
- 1 teaspoon rum flavoring
- 1 teaspoon lemon flavoring
- 1 teaspoon vanilla flavoring
- 1 1/2 teaspoons coconut flavoring

Direction

- Cream butter, shortening, and sugar until light and fluffy.
- Add beaten eggs.
- Sift flour and baking powder and add to cream mixture alternating with milk.
- Stir in flavors.
- Spoon into a well-greased pan.
- Bake at 350 for about 1 1/2 to 1 3/4 hours.

Nutrition Information

- Calories: 674.8
- Total Fat: 32.2
- Sodium: 227.6
- Sugar: 61.3
- Protein: 8
- Saturated Fat: 15.5
- Fiber: 1
- Total Carbohydrate: 90
- Cholesterol: 144.2

65. Fresh Orange Pound Cake

Serving: 1 cake, 12 serving(s) | Prep: 15mins | Ready in:

Ingredients

- 1 1/2 cups flour
- 1 1/2 cups sugar
- 1 tablespoon baking powder
- 3/4 cup butter
- 3/4 teaspoon salt
- 1 tablespoon vanilla extract
- 1 cup sour cream
- 1/2 cup cream cheese
- 3 eggs
- 1 orange, zest of
- 1 orange, juice of

Direction

- Preheat oven to 350 degrees.
- Combine flour, sugar, baking powder, orange zest, and salt and mix.
- Mix in butter, sour cream, cream cheese, orange juice, vanilla extract, and eggs.
- Bake for 50-60 minutes.
- Optional: Glaze the finished cake with either glaze made from powdered sugar and orange juice, or pour chocolate sauce over the cooled cake.

Nutrition Information

- Calories: 350.2
- Total Fat: 20
- Sodium: 402.3
- Fiber: 0.4
- Sugar: 26.8
- Protein: 4.3
- Saturated Fat: 11.8
- Total Carbohydrate: 39.1
- Cholesterol: 97.6

66. Fruit Cocktail Pound Cake

Serving: 10-12 serving(s) | Prep: 30mins | Ready in:

Ingredients

- 2 cups all-purpose white flour
- 1 teaspoon baking powder
- 1/8 teaspoon salt
- 1/4 cup white sugar
- 2 eggs
- 1/2 cup of softened butter or 1/2 cup margarine
- 1 1/2 teaspoons vanilla extract or 1 1/2 teaspoons amaretto liqueur
- 1/2 cup milk
- 1/2 cup fruit cocktail, juice from the can
- 1 (28 ounce) can fruit cocktail in heavy syrup, drained (collect the juice to add to milk)
- icing sugar, to garnish cake

Direction

- Preheat oven to 350°F.
- In a large mixing bowl cream together the softened margarine and the sugar.
- Mix well till creamy smooth. Add one egg at a time and beat after each addition.
- In a measuring glass combine the milk, the fruit cocktail juice and the vanilla extract (or amaretto liqueur).
- In a separate mixing bowl sift the flour, baking powder and salt together.

- Add 1/4 of the flour mix to the creamy butter mixture alternately with a little of the liquid; mix well after each addition. Keep doing this till there is no more flour or liquid left. Your cake batter should be rich and smooth/ If needed, add a tablespoon or more milk or juice--not too much, you don't want your cake watery.
- Fold in the drained fruit cocktail to your batter and mix well till all fruit is coated and not floating on top of batter.
- Pour the batter into two well-greased and lightly floured loaf pans or a Bundt cake pan.
- If using non-stick pans then just spray with a little oil spray.
- Bake for 40 to 50 minutes for loaf pans or till lightly golden brown and insert toothpick comes out clean. If baking in Bundt pan, it should be about the same time.
- Remove cake from oven and let sit on cake rack. Remove cake from pans and place on serving dish.
- Put icing sugar in sieve and tap side of sieve to get a light dusting all over top of cake.
- Serve cake slices with whipped cream or ice cream, makes a yummy light dessert.
- Note: you can do a summer berry cake by adding fresh fruit like blueberries, raspberries, strawberries, diced peaches, pears, and or nectarines.
- When making the fresh berry cake use either 1/2 cup of fruit cocktail juice + 1/cup milk OR use 1 cup of milk, but if you're replacing the juice with the whole cup of milk you will need to add 1/3 cup more sugar.

Nutrition Information

- Calories: 248.7
- Total Carbohydrate: 33.3
- Cholesterol: 68.4
- Sodium: 154.1
- Fiber: 1.1
- Sugar: 13.2
- Protein: 4.5
- Total Fat: 10.9

- Saturated Fat: 6.5

67. Fruit Pound Cake

Serving: 1 cake | Prep: 20mins | Ready in:

Ingredients

- 1 cup shortening
- 1 1/2 cups sugar
- 5 eggs
- 2 cups all-purpose flour
- 1 1/2 teaspoons salt
- 1/8 teaspoon mace
- 1 teaspoon vanilla
- 1/2 cup seedless raisin
- 1/3 cup cherries, from a jar, chopped
- 1/4 cup orange rind, grated
- 1/4 lemon, rind of, grated
- 1/4 cup nuts, chopped

Direction

- Cream shortening and sugar together.
- Add eggs, 1 at a time, beating after each addition.
- Add flour, salt, mace. Mix again.
- Add vanilla and beat. Add remaining ingredients and mix very well.
- Bake in a greased loaf pan for 60 -80 minutes with the oven temp set at 350*.
- **NOTE: To make a basic pound cake, the use above recipe, OMITTING the fruit and follow directions for baking/preparing. **

Nutrition Information

- Calories: 4735.6
- Total Fat: 250.2
- Sodium: 4081.6
- Fiber: 16.1
- Total Carbohydrate: 573.1
- Saturated Fat: 61.8
- Sugar: 353.6

- Cholesterol: 1057.5
- Protein: 66.3

68. German Chocolate Pound Cake

Serving: 16 serving(s) | Prep: 20mins | Ready in:

Ingredients

- 1 cup vegetable shortening
- 2 cups sugar
- 4 eggs
- 2 teaspoons vanilla extract
- 3 cups all-purpose flour
- 1/2 teaspoon baking soda
- 1 teaspoon salt
- 1 cup buttermilk
- 4 ounces unsweetened baking chocolate, melted
- Glaze Ingredients
- 2 unsweetened chocolate squares
- 2 tablespoons butter
- 1 cup confectioners' sugar
- 2 -3 tablespoons water

Direction

- Preheat oven to 300 degrees.
- Grease and flour a 10-inch tube pan or Bundt pan.
- Cream shortening at medium speed of mixer.
- Gradually add sugar until well mixed.
- Add eggs one at a time, beating well after each egg.
- Blend in vanilla extract.
- Combine flour, baking soda and salt.
- Add alternately with buttermilk to the creamed mixture.
- Continue mixing well.
- Mix in the melted chocolate last.
- Pour batter into prepared pan and bake for about 90 minutes or until cake tests done.
- Cool cake in pan on rack for about ten minutes, then turn out and let cake cool completely.

- You may sprinkle with confectioners' sugar or top with chocolate glaze.
- For glaze, microwave chocolate and butter together, in a medium sized bowl, until melted.
- Mix in confectioners' sugar and just enough water to make a smooth glaze.
- Pour glaze over cake and let trickle down the sides.

Nutrition Information

- Calories: 417.7
- Total Fat: 21.6
- Sodium: 231.7
- Protein: 5.9
- Saturated Fat: 8.6
- Fiber: 2.4
- Sugar: 33.4
- Total Carbohydrate: 54.5
- Cholesterol: 57.3

69. Gina's Sinsational Chocolate Pound Cake

Serving: 8 , 8 serving(s) | Prep: 0S | Ready in:

Ingredients

- 1 cup unsalted butter, room temperature, plus more for pan
- 1/2 cup Dutch-processed cocoa powder, plus more for pan
- 3 cups sugar
- 5 eggs, yolk
- 1 egg yolk
- 2 3/4 cups all-purpose flour
- 3/4 teaspoon table salt
- 1/2 teaspoon baking powder
- 2 teaspoons vanilla extract

Direction

- Preheat oven to 350 degrees F. Butter a 10-inch Bundt pan and dust with cocoa powder.
- In a large bowl of a stand mixer, add the butter and the sugar. Using the paddle attachment, cream together until light and fluffy and the volume has increased. Add the eggs and egg yolk, 1 at a time, beating after each addition.
- In another mixing bowl, whisk together the flour, cocoa powder, the salt, and baking powder.
- Add the dry ingredients alternatively with the buttermilk to the butter and egg mixture ending with the flour. Stir in the vanilla and pour the batter into the prepared Bundt pan. Bake for 1 hour and 10 minutes or until a toothpick inserted in the cake comes out clean. Let cool on a wire rack before turning out onto a serving plate and slicing.
- Glaze:
- Add the chocolate to a medium-sized bowl. In a small saucepan over low heat, add the cream and bring to a low simmer. Pour the cream over the chocolate and add the corn syrup. Once the chocolate melts, whisk together to combine. Drizzle over the cake and serve.

Nutrition Information

- Calories: 717.7
- Sugar: 75.5
- Cholesterol: 216.8
- Protein: 10
- Total Fat: 27.8
- Fiber: 3
- Saturated Fat: 16.2
- Sodium: 290.6
- Total Carbohydrate: 111.2

70. Gingerbread Pound Cake

Serving: 10 inch cake | Prep: 15mins | Ready in:

Ingredients

- 1 cup softened butter or 1 cup margarine
- 1 cup sugar
- 5 eggs
- 2 cups all-purpose flour
- 1/2 teaspoon baking soda
- 1 teaspoon ground ginger
- 1 teaspoon ground cinnamon
- 1 teaspoon ground cloves
- 1 cup molasses
- 1/2 cup sour cream
- sifted powdered sugar
- Lemon Sauce
- 1/2 cup sugar (optional)
- 2 tablespoons cornstarch (optional)
- 1 cup water (optional)
- 1 tablespoon butter or 1 tablespoon margarine (optional)
- 2 teaspoons grated fresh lemon rind (optional)
- 1/3 cup lemon juice (optional)

Direction

- In a mixing bowl, cream butter beating well on medium speed with an electric mixer; gradually add sugar.
- Add eggs, one at a time, beating after each egg is added.
- Combine flour, soda, and spices; set aside.
- Combine molasses and sour cream.
- Add flour mixture to creamed mixture alternately with molasses mixture, beginning and ending with flour mixture.
- Mix just until blended after each addition.
- Pour batter into a greased and floured 10 inch Bundt pan.
- Bake at 325 degrees for 1 hour or until wooden pick inserted in center comes out clean.
- Cool in pan for 15 minutes then remove and cool completely on a wire cake rack.
- Sprinkle with powdered sugar.
- Serve with Lemon sauce, if desired.
- Lemon Sauce: Combine first 3 ingredients in a saucepan, stirring until smooth.
- Cook over medium heat, stirring until smooth and thickened.
- Add remaining ingredients; cook until heated.

Nutrition Information

- Calories: 499
- Total Fat: 24.5
- Saturated Fat: 14.6
- Sugar: 39.2
- Protein: 6.2
- Sodium: 293.6
- Fiber: 0.9
- Total Carbohydrate: 65.3
- Cholesterol: 150.8

71. Glazed Apple Cider Pound Cake

Serving: 1 cake | Prep: 15mins | Ready in:

Ingredients

- CAKE
- 1 cup margarine
- 1/2 cup shortening
- 3 cups sugar
- 6 large eggs
- 3 cups flour
- 1/2 teaspoon salt
- 1/2 teaspoon baking powder
- 1/2 teaspoon allspice
- 3/4 teaspoon cinnamon
- 1/2 teaspoon nutmeg
- 1/4 teaspoon ground cloves
- 1 cup apple cider
- 1 teaspoon vanilla
- CARAMEL GLAZE
- 1/2 cup sugar
- 1/2 teaspoon baking soda
- 1/4 cup margarine
- 1/4 cup buttermilk
- 1/4 cup dark corn syrup
- 1 teaspoon vanilla

Direction

- CAKE: Soften margarine and shortening.
- Add sugar.
- Beat 10 minutes with mixer at medium speed.
- Add eggs one at a time.
- Add other ingredients.
- Beat well.
- Bake in a large tube pan at 325 for 90 minutes.
- GLAZE: Combine all ingredients and boil for 10 minutes.
- Drizzle over cake while cake is still warm.

Nutrition Information

- Calories: 6726.9
- Total Carbohydrate: 1061.6
- Total Fat: 249.6
- Saturated Fat: 59.9
- Sodium: 3974.3
- Fiber: 11.8
- Sugar: 727
- Cholesterol: 1118.5
- Protein: 80

72. Grandma's Butternut Pound Cake

Serving: 1 cake | Prep: 10mins | Ready in:

Ingredients

- 1 cup Butter Flavor Crisco
- 1 cup milk
- 2 cups sugar
- 5 eggs
- 1/2 cup self rising flour
- 2 1/2 cups cake flour
- 2 tablespoons butternut flavoring

Direction

- Cream Crisco, sugar and eggs together.
- Beat on high speed for 5 minutes.
- Then add milk and flour on low speed until mixed well.
- Add butternut flavoring and bake in tube or Bundt pan for 1 hour and 15 minutes at 300 degrees F.

- Frost with Butternut frosting if desired.
- See my recipes for the frosting recipe!
- May be baked in 3 layer pans also.

Nutrition Information

- Calories: 5377.8
- Fiber: 7.5
- Sugar: 402.8
- Total Carbohydrate: 726.8
- Cholesterol: 1206.5
- Total Fat: 242.3
- Saturated Fat: 96.5
- Sodium: 1270.2
- Protein: 73.7

73. Grandma's Original Pound Cake

Serving: 8-12 serving(s) | Prep: 30mins | Ready in:

Ingredients

- 1 cup butter
- 2 cups sugar
- 4 eggs, separated
- 1/2 teaspoon salt
- 1 lemon, rind of
- 2 1/2 cups flour
- 2 1/2 teaspoons baking powder
- 1 cup milk

Direction

- Heat oven to 350 degrees. Grease a tube pan or Bundt pan.
- In mixing bowl, cream butter and sugar. Add egg yolks and lemon rind.
- Sift together flour and baking powder and add to creamed mixture alternating with milk.
- In separate bowl, beat egg whites and salt until stiff. Mix some of whites into batter, and then fold batter into remaining whites.

- Pour into pan and bake for 30-45 mins, until it tests as done.

Nutrition Information

- Calories: 596.1
- Sodium: 473
- Total Carbohydrate: 81.8
- Protein: 8.4
- Total Fat: 27
- Saturated Fat: 16.1
- Fiber: 1.1
- Sugar: 50.3
- Cholesterol: 171

74. Granny's Pound Cake

Serving: 1 cake | Prep: 15mins | Ready in:

Ingredients

- 1 1/2 cups butter
- 1 box powdered sugar, sifted
- 6 eggs
- 1 teaspoon vanilla extract (or choice of flavor)
- 3 cups all-purpose flour

Direction

- In LARGE bowl, cream butter and sugar.
- Add eggs, one at a time, and beat well.
- Slowly add flour and flavoring beat for 5 minutes.
- Pour into greased and floured tube or Bundt pan.
- Bake at 300° for 1 hour and 45 minutes.

Nutrition Information

- Calories: 5725.2
- Saturated Fat: 184.9
- Sugar: 373
- Total Carbohydrate: 664.5
- Cholesterol: 2001.1

- Protein: 79.4
- Total Fat: 310.1
- Sodium: 2392.9
- Fiber: 10.1

- Protein: 0.1
- Total Fat: 11.5
- Sodium: 81.8
- Sugar: 0.6
- Cholesterol: 30.5

75. Griddled Pound Cake With Lemon Curd

Serving: 4 serving(s) | Prep: 10mins | Ready in:

Ingredients

- 4 slices dense butter pound cake, each 3/4-inch thick
- 4 tablespoons butter, at room temperature
- 2 tablespoons lemon curd
- 1 teaspoon powdered sugar
- 4 sprigs mint

Direction

- Butter both sides of each pound-cake slice. Heat a wide, heavy-bottomed frying pan or flat griddle pan over medium heat for 1 minute. Place the slices in the pan, and cook for 1½ minutes, then flip and cook for 1 minute on the other side.
- Remove to a cutting board, and cut each slice in half.
- Place each slice on an individual plate with a dollop of lemon curd. Sprinkle with powdered sugar, and garnish with a mint sprig.
- You can make this with frozen pound cake too.
- Just slice it straight out of the freezer, and cook for 2 minutes on the first side and 1¼ minutes on the other.

Nutrition Information

- Calories: 104.2
- Saturated Fat: 7.3
- Fiber: 0
- Total Carbohydrate: 0.6

76. Grilled Pound Cake; Mexican Chocolate Sauce Tropical Fruit

Serving: 6 serving(s) | Prep: 35mins | Ready in:

Ingredients

- WHIPPED CREAM
- 1 cup heavy cream
- 3 tablespoons confectioners' sugar
- 1 tablespoon dark rum
- 1/2 teaspoon pure vanilla extract
- MEXICAN CHOCOLATE SAUCE
- 3/4 cup heavy cream
- 1/2 teaspoon ground cinnamon
- 1/2 teaspoon pure dried ancho chile powder
- 1 cup semi-sweet chocolate chips
- 1/2 teaspoon pure vanilla extract
- FRUIT SALAD
- 1 large mango (peeled and cut into 1/3-inch wedges)
- 1 medium papaya, halved (seeded, peeled and cut into 1/3-inch wedges)
- 1 tablespoon coarsely chopped fresh basil
- 1 teaspoon pure vanilla extract
- POUND CAKE
- 2 tablespoons unsalted butter, softened
- 6 slices homemade butter pound cake (1 1/4-inch) or 6 slices fresh bakery butter pound cake (1 1/4-inch)
- 3 tablespoons toasted sliced almonds (to garnish) or 3 tablespoons toasted macadamia nuts, chopped (to garnish)

Direction

- MAKE THE WHIPPED CREAM:

- In a medium bowl, using an electric mixer, softly whip the heavy cream.
- Add the confectioners' sugar, rum and vanilla and whip the cream until firm peaks form.
- Refrigerate the whipped cream.
- MAKE THE CHOCOLATE SAUCE:
- In a medium saucepan, bring the heavy cream to a simmer over moderately high heat with the cinnamon and chile powder.
- Add the chocolate chips and vanilla.
- Remove from the heat and let stand for 1 minute, then whisk to blend; keep warm.
- MAKE THE FRUIT SALAD:
- In a medium bowl, toss the mango and papaya with the basil and vanilla.
- PREPARE THE POUND CAKE:
- Light a grill or preheat a grill pan.
- Butter both sides of the pound cake slices.
- Grill the pound cake over moderate heat, turning once, until golden, about 2 minutes per side.
- Set a slice of grilled pound cake on each of 6 plates and top each one with 3 tablespoons of the warm chocolate sauce and the fruit salad.
- Top each serving with a dollop of the rum whipped cream and sprinkle with the toasted almonds.
- Pass the remaining chocolate sauce at the table.
- **MAKE AHEAD: The whipped cream and fruit salad can be refrigerated for up to 4 hours; whip the cream gently before serving. The chocolate sauce can be refrigerated for up to 2 days; rewarm before serving.

Nutrition Information

- Calories: 737.9
- Total Fat: 60.9
- Sugar: 30.7
- Total Carbohydrate: 44.4
- Protein: 12.7
- Saturated Fat: 25.2
- Sodium: 35.2
- Fiber: 8.6
- Cholesterol: 105.3

77. Grilled Rum Pound Cake With Fruit Sauce

Serving: 1 1/2 Cups, 4-6 serving(s) | Prep: 10mins | Ready in:

Ingredients

- 4 slices lb cake (1 1/2-inch thick)
- 1 cup spiced rum
- 1/4 teaspoon ground ginger
- 1 tablespoon brown sugar
- 1/3 cup sugar
- 2 cups fruit (or 1 -10-12 oz bag of frozen)
- 1 tablespoon water
- 1 teaspoon cornstarch

Direction

- Rum liquid -- In a pie plate, or small flat bowl, mix the rum, ginger, and brown sugar. Brush on or lightly dip the pound cake into the rum marinade.
- Fruit sauce -- In a medium bowl, add 1 10 oz. bag of frozen berries or any of your favorite fruits, cut up (2 cups). Add 1/4-1/2 cup sugar depending on how sweet you like the sauce, corn starch, water and cover with saran wrap. Cook in the microwave on medium high until the berries or fruit is soft and begins to break down. Depending on your microwave, it will take about 5 minutes on high.
- Pound cake -- Grill the pound cake, outside grill or inside grill pan and then top with the fruit sauce.
- Garnishes -- could be mascarpone cheese, whipped cream, chopped nuts.

Nutrition Information

- Calories: 208.8
- Total Fat: 0
- Saturated Fat: 0

- Sodium: 2.1
- Fiber: 0
- Sugar: 20
- Cholesterol: 0
- Protein: 0
- Total Carbohydrate: 20.7

78. Grocery Store Gossip Pound Cake

Serving: 1 9x13 cake pan, 12 serving(s) | Prep: 5mins | Ready in:

Ingredients

- 1 regular box cake mix (great with yellow)
- 1 cup sour cream
- 1/2 cup sugar
- 3/4 cup oil
- 5 eggs
- 1 teaspoon vanilla

Direction

- Preheat oven to 350 degrees.
- In large mixing bowl, combine all ingredients together.
- Beat on medium speed for approximately two minutes.
- Pour into greased 9x13 cake pan, spread evenly.
- Bake 20-30 minutes at 350 degrees.
- Cake will spring back when done.
- It is great brushed lightly with melted butter or your favorite icing!

Nutrition Information

- Calories: 225.3
- Saturated Fat: 4.9
- Fiber: 0
- Sugar: 8.6
- Total Carbohydrate: 9.3
- Protein: 3.2

- Total Fat: 19.7
- Sodium: 39.4
- Cholesterol: 96.6

79. Hazelnut Pound Cake With Fresh Raspberries

Serving: 12 serving(s) | Prep: 20mins | Ready in:

Ingredients

- 1 cup hazelnuts
- 1 cup yellow cornmeal
- 1 cup unsalted butter
- 1 cup sugar
- 1/2 teaspoon salt
- 1/2 teaspoon vanilla extract
- 4 large eggs, separated
- 1 cup all-purpose flour
- 1 pint fresh raspberry

Direction

- Heat oven to 350 degrees. Butter a 9-inch Bundt or tube pan.
- Toast nuts on baking sheet until fragrant and browned, 15-20 minutes. Rub nuts in kitchen towel to remove as much skin as possible.
- Process nuts and cornmeal in food processor until very finely ground, about 2 minutes.
- Beat butter, sugar, salt, and vanilla in bowl until light and fluffy. Add egg yolks and mix until blended. Mix in nut mixture, then gently stir in flour with rubber spatula.
- Beat egg whites in clean bowl until stiff peaks form (but not too dry). Add 1/3 of the whites to batter and gently fold with spatula to lighten batter. Add remaining egg whites and gently fold until blended. Spoon batter into prepared pan.
- Bake cake until wooden pick inserted into center comes out clean, about 1 hour. Let cool completely on wire rack.
- When ready to serve, invert cake onto platter. Slice and serve with fresh raspberries.

Nutrition Information

- Calories: 384
- Total Fat: 24.5
- Fiber: 3.8
- Sugar: 18.5
- Saturated Fat: 10.8
- Sodium: 126.3
- Total Carbohydrate: 37.6
- Cholesterol: 111.2
- Protein: 6.2

80. Honey Vanilla Pound Cake

Serving: 1 loaf, 4-6 serving(s) | Prep: 20mins | Ready in:

Ingredients

- 1/2 lb unsalted butter, at room temperature
- 1 1/4 cups sugar
- 4 extra large eggs, at room temperature
- 2 tablespoons honey
- 2 teaspoons pure vanilla extract
- 1 teaspoon grated lemon zest
- 1 3/4 cups sifted cake flour
- 1 teaspoon kosher salt
- 1/2 teaspoon baking powder

Direction

- Preheat oven to 325°F.
- Grease and flour an 8 1/2 x 41/2 x 2 1/2 inch loaf pan. Line the bottom with parchment paper.
- In a mixing bowl using an electric mixer cream the butter and sugar on medium speed for 3 to 4 minutes, until light. In a glass measuring cup combine the eggs, honey, vanilla and lemon zest. Combine egg mixture to butter cream slowly making sure eggs mix completely and scraping sides of bowl as you mix eggs.
- Sift together the flour, salt, and baking powder. With the mixer on low speed, add

flour mixture to butter and egg mixture very slowly just until combined. Finish mixing batter with a rubber spatula and pour into prepared baking pan. Smooth the top, bake for 50 to 60 minutes until toothpick inserted in center comes out clean.

Nutrition Information

- Calories: 989.5
- Sodium: 570.7
- Total Carbohydrate: 118.9
- Protein: 12.7
- Total Fat: 52.3
- Saturated Fat: 31
- Fiber: 1.1
- Sugar: 72
- Cholesterol: 367.4

81. Inez's Sour Cream Pound Cake

Serving: 1 cake | Prep: 25mins | Ready in:

Ingredients

- 1/2 cup butter, softened
- 1/2 cup shortening
- 3 cups sugar
- 6 eggs
- 3 cups sifted flour
- 1/4 teaspoon baking powder
- 1/4 teaspoon baking soda
- 1/4 teaspoon salt
- 1 (8 ounce) carton sour cream
- 2 -3 teaspoons vanilla or 2 -3 teaspoons lemon extract or 2 -3 teaspoons almond extract

Direction

- Cream butter, shortening and sugar.
- Gradually add eggs one at a time, beating well after each addition.
- In another bowl, combine flour, baking powder, baking soda and salt.

- Add to creamed mixture, alternating with sour cream. Begin and end with flour mixture.
- Add vanilla, lemon or almond extract just mixing enough to blend.
- Pour batter into a greased and floured 10 inch tube pan.
- Bake at 325 for 1 1/2 hours or until wooden pick comes out clean.
- Cool 10 minutes and remove from pan.

Nutrition Information

- Calories: 6383.5
- Fiber: 10.1
- Cholesterol: 1618.3
- Sugar: 604.3
- Total Carbohydrate: 900
- Protein: 85
- Total Fat: 278.1
- Saturated Fat: 125
- Sodium: 2195.6

82. Junior's Pound Cake

Serving: 2 loaf cakes | Prep: 45mins | Ready in:

Ingredients

- 3 1/4 cups cake flour
- 1 teaspoon baking powder
- 1 teaspoon salt
- 1/4 teaspoon nutmeg
- 1 cup unsalted butter, at room temperature
- 1 cup shortening
- 2 cups sugar
- 9 extra large eggs
- 2 tablespoons pure vanilla extract
- 3/4 cup milk

Direction

- Place a rack in the middle of the oven and preheat the oven to 325°.
- Butter 2 loaf pans (9x5x3 x 2 1/4-inch), then line the bottoms with parchment or wax paper.
- Sift the cake flour, baking powder, salt, and nutmeg together into a medium-size bowl and set aside.
- Cream the butter and shortening in a large bowl with an electric mixer on high until light yellow, about 5 minutes.
- Then, while the mixer is still running, add the sugar, about 1/2 cup at a time, beating 1 to 2 minutes after each addition.
- Now add the eggs, one at a time, beating 3 minutes after adding each one.
- Beat the batter until it is light yellow, airy, and starts crawling up the sides of the bowl, a total of about 35 minutes in all. (This is important)
- Beat in the vanilla.
- Sift about one fourth of the flour mixture over the batter and stir it in by hand, then stir in one third of the milk.
- Repeat by adding one-quarter more flour, one third more milk, another one fourth of the flour, then the rest of the milk.
- Finally, stir in the rest of the flour.
- Stir after each addition until the ingredients are well incorporated.
- Gently spoon half of the batter into each loaf pan.
- Set the 2 pans side by side in the oven, making sure they are not touching each other.
- Bake the cakes until the tops are golden and the center of each cake springs back when you touch it lightly and a toothpick inserted in the center comes out with moist crumbs (not batter) clinging to it, about 1 hour.
- Let the cakes cool on a wire rack for 30 minutes before removing them from the pans.
- Note: I am assuming that the 35 minutes total beating time includes all additions to the batter as well.

Nutrition Information

- Calories: 3781.1
- Saturated Fat: 94.4

- Sodium: 1772.7
- Sugar: 204.3
- Total Carbohydrate: 382.4
- Protein: 55.1
- Total Fat: 225.8
- Fiber: 3.9
- Cholesterol: 1360.9

83. Kentucky Pound Cake

Serving: 2 loaves, 10-12 serving(s) | Prep: 10mins | Ready in:

Ingredients

- 2 cups sugar
- 2 cups self rising flour (I make my own, never buy it)
- 4 eggs
- 2 cups whipping cream
- 1 teaspoon vanilla
- 1/4 tsp. lemon oil

Direction

- Grease and flour Bundt pan or 2 loaf pans. (I use Pam Baking Spray).
- Heat oven to 350. Beat all ingredients on low for one minute. Pour into pan(s). Bake for 45 minutes, checking often towards the end. Let sit in pan for 10 min. Unmold, let cool completely. This is best the next day, after a night wrapped in cling wrap, and placed in fridge.

Nutrition Information

- Calories: 437.3
- Saturated Fat: 11.6
- Sugar: 40.1
- Cholesterol: 139.6
- Protein: 6
- Total Fat: 19.8
- Sodium: 364.4

- Fiber: 0.7
- Total Carbohydrate: 60.1

84. Key Lime Pound Cake

Serving: 1 cake, 12 serving(s) | Prep: 20mins | Ready in:

Ingredients

- 2 cups sugar
- 1 cup butter or 1 cup margarine, at room temperature
- 2 teaspoons key lime juice (Floribbean brand)
- 2 teaspoons lime rind, finely grated
- 1 teaspoon vanilla
- 5 eggs, beaten
- 1/4 cup sour cream
- 2 cups flour
- 1/2 teaspoon baking soda
- 1/2 cup confectioners' sugar
- 1 teaspoon key lime juice

Direction

- Preheat oven to 350 degrees (F).
- In a large bowl, using an electric mixer, cream together the sugar and butter.
- Beat until light and fluffy.
- Add key lime juice, lime rind and vanilla.
- Add one egg at a time, mixing well after each addition.
- Mix in sour cream.
- Sift in flour and baking soda.
- Mix to blend thoroughly.
- Spoon batter into a greased 10" Bundt pan or tube pan.
- Bake for 60-65 minutes, or until a skewer inserted into the center comes out clean.
- Cool on a wire rack for 15-20 minutes before turning cake out of pan.
- Meanwhile, make the glaze by combining confectioners' sugar and key lime juice.
- Mix until smooth.
- Pour glaze over warm cake.
- Let cool completely before serving.

Nutrition Information

- Calories: 400.3
- Sugar: 38.5
- Total Carbohydrate: 54.7
- Cholesterol: 120.7
- Total Fat: 18.5
- Saturated Fat: 10.9
- Sodium: 221.8
- Fiber: 0.6
- Protein: 5

85. Laird's Applejack Pound Cake

Serving: 10-12 serving(s) | Prep: 30mins | Ready in:

Ingredients

- 1 lb butter
- 3 cups sugar
- 8 eggs, separated
- 3 cups sifted flour
- 2 teaspoons vanilla
- 1/3 cup Applejack
- 1/2 cup chopped pecans

Direction

- Cream butter 2 cups sugar 'til light and fluffy.
- Add yolks one at a time, mixing well each time. Add flour alternately with vanilla and applejack in thirds, beating until smooth after each addition.
- In another bowl, beat egg whites until stiff but not dry.
- Beat remaining sugar into egg whites gradually. Gently fold egg yolk mixture into whites.
- Sprinkle nuts on bottom of well buttered 10" tube pan.
- Carefully turn batter into pan.
- Bake in 350 oven for approximately 11/2 hours.

- Cool completely and remove from pan.

Nutrition Information

- Calories: 793.1
- Sugar: 60.7
- Protein: 9.8
- Sodium: 318.3
- Fiber: 1.5
- Saturated Fat: 25
- Total Carbohydrate: 89.8
- Cholesterol: 266.8
- Total Fat: 45.1

86. Latte Pound Cake

Serving: 16 serving(s) | Prep: 15mins | Ready in:

Ingredients

- 5 tablespoons instant coffee
- 1/2 cup hot milk
- 1 1/2 cups sugar or 45 (1 g) packets Equal sugar substitute
- 1 1/3 cups butter (softened)
- 4 eggs
- 2 2/3 cups flour
- 3 teaspoons baking powder
- 1/2 teaspoon salt
- 1 cup chopped pecans

Direction

- Preheat oven to 325 degrees F. Grease and flour Bundt pan.
- In a small bowl combine coffee and hot milk and set aside.
- In a food processor or large mixing bowl, mix sugar and butter until light and fluffy. Add eggs one at a time, mixing well after each addition.
- Mix in Flour, baking powder, salt and coffee mixture, mix well.

- Fold in nuts, pour into prepared pan, bake at 325 for 60 to 70 minutes or until a toothpick inserted in center of cake comes out clean.
- Cool completely on a wire rack.
- Cinnamon or Vanilla Icing.
- In a small bowl combine 1 cup confectioner's sugar, 1/4 teaspoon cinnamon or vanilla (your choice). Stir enough milk (4-5 teaspoons) to thin icing to drizzle consistency. Drizzle over cooled cake.

Nutrition Information

- Calories: 358.8
- Protein: 5
- Saturated Fat: 10.7
- Sodium: 272
- Sugar: 19.2
- Cholesterol: 94.6
- Total Fat: 22
- Fiber: 1.2
- Total Carbohydrate: 37

87. Leila's Easy Chocolate Pound Cake

Serving: 16 serving(s) | Prep: 15mins | Ready in:

Ingredients

- 1 cup all-purpose flour, plus flour for dusting the tube pan
- 1 (18 1/4 ounce) packageplain devil's food cake mix
- 1 cup unsalted butter, at room temperature
- 1 cup granulated sugar
- 1 (8 ounce) can Hersheys Chocolate Syrup
- 6 large eggs
- 1/2 cup water
- 2 teaspoons confectioners' sugar, for dusting the cake

Direction

- Place a rack in the center of the oven and preheat the oven to 350 degrees. Lightly mist a 10-inch tube pan with vegetable oil spray and dust it with flour. Shake out the excess flour. Set the tube pan aside.
- Place the cake mix, flour, butter, granulated sugar, chocolate syrup, 1 egg, and 1/2 cup of water in a large mixing bowl. Beat with an electric mixer on low speed for 30 seconds.
- Add the remaining eggs one at a time, beating on low speed until each is incorporated, stopping in between to scrape down the side of the bowl with a rubber spatula.
- When all of the eggs have been added, increase the mixer speed to medium and beat the batter 1 minute longer, scraping down the side of the bowl again if needed. The batter should look smooth and thick. Transfer the batter to the prepared tube pan, smoothing the top with a rubber spatula.
- Bake the cake until the top springs back when lightly pressed with a finger, 50 to 55 minutes. Transfer the tube pan to a wire rack and let the cake cool for about 20 minutes.
- Run a long, sharp knife around the edges of the cake and invert it onto a wire rack, then invert it again onto another wire rack so that the cake is right side up. Let the cake cool completely, about 20 minutes. Dust the cake with confectioner's sugar or top it with a chocolate glaze.

Nutrition Information

- Calories: 385.3
- Saturated Fat: 9
- Sodium: 305.1
- Fiber: 1.4
- Sugar: 32.4
- Cholesterol: 109.8
- Total Fat: 18.6
- Protein: 5.5
- Total Carbohydrate: 51.8

88. Lemon Blueberry Pound Cake

Serving: 1 bundt cake, 12-16 serving(s) | Prep: 10mins | Ready in:

Ingredients

- 1 (18 1/2 ounce) box lemon cake mix (see note below)
- 1 (3 1/2 ounce) box instant lemon pudding mix
- 1/4 cup granulated sugar
- 1/2 cup water
- 3/4 cup vegetable oil
- 3 large eggs
- 8 ounces cream cheese, at room temperature
- 1 (16 1/2 ounce) can blueberries, rinsed and drained well
- GLAZE
- 1 cup confectioners' sugar
- 2 tablespoons fresh lemon juice

Direction

- NOTE-I use Duncan Hines because they do not have pudding in the mix as do the Betty Crocker and Pillsbury brands.
- If you are using another brand, make sure it does not have pudding already in the mix or the texture may not be the same.
- Preheat oven to 350.
- Grease and flour a 10-inch Bundt pan (or use Baker's Joy as I do).
- In a large bowl, stir together the cake mix, pudding mix and sugar.
- Make a well in the centre and add the water, oil, eggs and cream cheese.
- Beat on low speed until blended.
- Scrape bowl.
- Beat on medium speed for 2 minutes.
- (This will be a fairly thick batter.) Gently stir in the blueberries.
- Pour batter into prepared pan.
- Bake for 50 to 60 minutes, or until top is golden brown and cake tester inserted in centre comes out clean.
- Let cool in pan 10 minutes, then turn out on wire rack and cool completely.
- GLAZE: In a small bowl, combine sugar and lemon juice to make light glaze.
- Drizzle over cooled cake.
- This is not a heavy glaze.

Nutrition Information

- Calories: 501.8
- Fiber: 1.4
- Total Carbohydrate: 62.4
- Protein: 5.2
- Saturated Fat: 7.1
- Sodium: 468.1
- Sugar: 37
- Cholesterol: 74.5
- Total Fat: 26.7

89. Lemon Coconut Pound Cake (Vegan)

Serving: 1 loaf, 10 serving(s) | Prep: 30mins | Ready in:

Ingredients

- 1 cup tofu (use Mori-nu silken tofu firm style-I blended it before mixing it with the wet ingredients)
- 3/4 cup coconut milk
- 1 cup sugar
- 1/3 cup canola oil
- 2 teaspoons vanilla
- 1 teaspoon lemon extract (or 1/4 tsp. lemon essential oil)
- 1/2 teaspoon coconut extract (optional)
- 2 cups flour (I used white spelt)
- 3 tablespoons arrowroot
- 1 1/2 teaspoons baking powder
- 1/2 teaspoon baking soda
- 1/2 teaspoon salt

Direction

- Preheat oven to 325'F.
- Oil and flour a 9 x 5 inch loaf pan.
- Take a cup of the silken tofu and blend it until smooth.
- In a medium bowl, using a hand mixer, blend the smooth tofu, coconut milk, sugar, oil, vanilla and lemon extract (and the coconut if using) until completely smooth.
- In a separate bowl, sift together all the dry ingredients. Fold the wet into the dry using a spoon (I used a spatula) and mix until just combined. Then using a hand mixer on low mix for 15-20 seconds, just to remove the lumps -- do not over mix!
- Pour the batter into your prepared loaf pan and smooth the top.
- Bake for 60-70 minutes until a skewer comes out clean in the center.
- Let cool in the pan about 10 minutes before removing. Then cool completely on a wire rack before slicing -- it will fall apart if you don't.
- Bon Appétit!

Nutrition Information

- Calories: 302.7
- Protein: 4.8
- Total Fat: 12.4
- Saturated Fat: 4.2
- Fiber: 1.3
- Total Carbohydrate: 43.8
- Sodium: 247.4
- Sugar: 21.7
- Cholesterol: 0

90. Lemon Delight Pound Cake

Serving: 8 slices, 8 serving(s) | Prep: 10mins | Ready in:

Ingredients

- 1 1/4 cups reduced-fat baking mix
- 2/3 cup sugar

- 1/3 cup orange juice
- 3 tablespoons vegetable oil
- 1 teaspoon lemon extract
- 2 egg whites
- FOR GLAZE
- 1/2 cup powdered sugar
- 4 teaspoons lemon juice

Direction

- Heat oven to 325.
- Generously grease and flour a loaf pan.
- In a medium bowl, combine the cake ingredients. Blend on low speed until moistened; beat 3 minutes at medium speed.
- Pour batter into prepared pan.
- Bake 30-35 minutes or until a toothpick comes out clean.
- After removing from oven, prick deeply with fork every inch or so.
- In a small bowl, blend glaze ingredients until smooth.
- Spoon a quarter of the glaze over the hot cake in the pan. Let stand 10 minutes.
- Invert onto a serving plate and spoon remaining glaze over cake.

Nutrition Information

- Calories: 149.6
- Total Fat: 5.1
- Fiber: 0
- Total Carbohydrate: 25.5
- Protein: 1
- Saturated Fat: 0.7
- Sodium: 13.9
- Sugar: 25
- Cholesterol: 0

91. Lemon Ginger Pound Cake

Serving: 6 serving(s) | Prep: 30mins | Ready in:

Ingredients

- FOR CAKE
- 3 tablespoons finely chopped peeled fresh ginger
- 3⁄4 cup granulated sugar, plus
- 2 tablespoons granulated sugar
- 1 cup all-purpose flour
- 1 teaspoon baking powder
- 1⁄4 teaspoon ground ginger
- 1⁄4 teaspoon salt
- 1⁄4 cup whole milk
- 1⁄2 teaspoon vanilla
- 1⁄2 cup unsalted butter, softened
- 2 tablespoons finely grated fresh lemon zest
- 2 large eggs
- 2 tablespoons fresh lemon juice
- FOR GLAZE
- 1⁄2 cup icing sugar
- 1 1⁄2 tablespoons fresh lemon juice

Direction

- Preheat oven to 325°F.
- Generously butter a 4 to 5 cup nonstick Bundt, kugelhopf or loaf pan, and then flour it, knocking out excess.
- Chill 10 minutes.
- Finely grind together fresh ginger and 1/4 cup sugar in a food processor (mixture will be wet).
- Whisk together flour, baking powder, ground ginger, and salt.
- Stir together milk and vanilla in a small bowl.
- Beat together butter, remaining 1/2 cup plus 2 TBS sugar, and zest in a large bowl with an electric mixer until fluffy.
- Add eggs 1 at a time, beating well after each addition.
- Alternately add flour and milk mixtures to butter and eggs in 4 batches, beginning with flour and mixing at low speed until each batch is just incorporated.
- Mix in ginger sugar until just combined, then lemon juice.
- Spoon batter into pan, smoothing top, and bake in middle of the oven until golden brown on top and a tester inserted into center comes

out clean, about 40 minutes (about 1 hour for loaf pan).
- Carefully loosen edges with a knife and immediately invert cake onto a rack to cool completely.
- Gradually add confectioners' sugar to 1 TBS lemon juice, whisking until smooth and adding more juice, 1 drop at a time, if glaze is too thick.
- Drizzle decoratively over top of cake.
- Serve to six very lucky friends or family members!

Nutrition Information

- Calories: 401.1
- Total Carbohydrate: 57.5
- Cholesterol: 112.2
- Protein: 4.9
- Total Fat: 17.6
- Fiber: 0.9
- Sugar: 40.1
- Saturated Fat: 10.5
- Sodium: 188.1

92. Lemon Pound Cake With Mixed Berries

Serving: 8 serving(s) | Prep: 20mins | Ready in:

Ingredients

- Cake
- cooking spray
- 2 teaspoons all-purpose flour
- 1 cup all-purpose flour
- 1⁄4 teaspoon baking powder
- 2⁄3 cup sugar
- 1⁄3 cup butter, softened
- 2 large egg whites
- 1 large egg
- 1 teaspoon lemon rind, grated
- 1 teaspoon lemon extract

- 1/4 cup low-fat vanilla yogurt
- Topping
- 1 cup strawberry, sliced
- 1/3 cup fresh blueberries
- 1 (10 ounce) package frozen raspberries, in syrup (thawed and undrained)
- 1 cup low-fat vanilla yogurt

Direction

- Preheat oven to 350 degrees F. Coat an 8 x 4 inch loaf pan with cooking spray; dust with 2 teaspoons flour.
- Lightly spoon 1 cup flour into a dry measuring cup; level with a knife. Combine 1 cup flour and baking powder; stirring with a whisk; set aside.
- Place sugar and butter in a large bowl; beat with a mixer at high speed until fluffy (about 2 minutes). Add egg whites and egg; beating well after each addition. Beat in rind and extract. Add flour mixture and 1/4 cup yogurt alternately to sugar mixture, beginning and ending with flour mixture; mix well after each addition. Spoon batter into prepared pan. Bake at 350 degrees for 45 minutes or until a wooden pick inserted in center comes out clean. Cool in pan 10 minutes on wire rack; remove from pan. Cool completely on wire rack.
- To prepare topping; combine berries, tossing well. Cut cake into 8 slices. Top each cake slice with 1/4 cup berry mixture and 2 tablespoons yogurt.

Nutrition Information

- Calories: 284.5
- Sodium: 127.8
- Fiber: 2.5
- Total Carbohydrate: 46.1
- Protein: 5.8
- Total Fat: 9
- Saturated Fat: 5.4
- Sugar: 31.3
- Cholesterol: 45.5

93. Lemon Pound Cake With Lemon Syrup

Serving: 8-12 serving(s) | Prep: 5mins | Ready in:

Ingredients

- 3/4 cup sugar
- 1/2 cup butter or 1/2 cup margarine, softened
- 1 cup sour cream
- 3 egg whites
- 1 tablespoon lemon juice
- 1 grated lemon, rind of
- 2 1/2 cups all-purpose flour
- 1 teaspoon baking soda
- fresh nutmeg
- Lemon Syrup
- 1/2 cup sugar
- 1/4 cup fresh lemon juice
- 1/4 cup water

Direction

- Beat the sugar and butter together until light and fluffy.
- Add the sour cream, egg whites, lemon juice, and lemon rind, and beat until smooth.
- Add the flour, baking soda, and nutmeg and beat until smooth.
- Pour into a greased and floured loaf pan.
- Bake in a preheated 350F oven for 40 to 50 minutes, until a toothpick inserted in the centre comes out clean.
- Cool on a wire rack.
- Spoon the warm lemon syrup over the cake, allowing it to soak in.
- Lemon Syrup: Combine all ingredients in a small saucepan and bring to a boil over moderate heat, stirring to dissolve the sugar.
- Cool slightly before pouring over cake.

Nutrition Information

- Calories: 435.2
- Total Fat: 17.9

- Fiber: 1.1
- Sugar: 31.7
- Cholesterol: 43.1
- Protein: 6.5
- Saturated Fat: 11.1
- Sodium: 275.8
- Total Carbohydrate: 63.2

94. Lemon Pound Cake(ATK)

Serving: 1 loaf, 8 serving(s) | Prep: 15mins | Ready in:

Ingredients

- Cake
- 16 tablespoons unsalted butter (2 sticks)
- 1 tablespoon unsalted butter, softened for the pan
- 1 1/2 cups cake flour (6 ounces)
- 1 tablespoon cake flour, for the pan
- 1 teaspoon baking powder
- 1/2 teaspoon salt
- 1 1/4 cups sugar (8 3/4 ounces)
- 2 tablespoons lemon zest
- 2 teaspoons lemons (1 lemon)
- 4 large eggs, room temperature
- 1 1/2 teaspoons vanilla
- glaze
- 1/2 cup sugar (3 1/2 ounces)
- 1/4 cup lemon juice (2 lemons)

Direction

- Adjust an oven rack to the middle position and heat the oven to 350 degrees. Grease an 8 1/2 by 4 1/2 inch loaf pan with 1 tablespoon of the softened butter; dust with 1 tablespoon of the flour, tapping our the excess. In a medium bowl, whisk together the remaining 1 1/2 cups flour, the baking powder and the salt; set aside.
- Melt the remaining 16 tablespoons butter in a small saucepan over medium heat. Whisk the melted butter thoroughly to reincorporate any separated milk solids.

- In a food processor, pulse the sugar and zest until combined, about 5 pulses. Add the lemon juice, eggs and vanilla; process until combined, about 5 seconds. With the machine running, add the melted butter through the feed tube in a steady stream [this should take about 20 seconds]. Transfer the mixture to a large bowl. Sift the flour mixture over the egg mixture in three additions, whisking gently after each addition until just combined.
- Pour the batter into the prepared pan and bake 15 minutes. Reduce the oven temperature to 325 degrees and continue to bake until deep golden brown and a toothpick inserted in the center comes out clean, about 35 minutes, rotating the pan halfway through the baking time. Cool in the pan for 10 minutes, then turn onto a wire rack. Pike the top and sides of the cake throughout with a toothpick. Cool to room temperature, at least 1 hour. [The cooled cake can be wrapped tightly in plastic wrap and stored at room temperature for 5 days.].
- For the glaze: While the cake is cooling, bring the sugar and lemon juice to a boil in a small saucepan, stirring occasionally to dissolve the sugar. Reduce the heat to low and simmer until thickened slightly, about 2 minutes. Brush the top and sides of the cake with the glaze and cool to room temperature.

Nutrition Information

- Calories: 523.1
- Sodium: 230.8
- Fiber: 0.6
- Total Carbohydrate: 65.8
- Total Fat: 27.1
- Cholesterol: 157.9
- Protein: 5.6
- Saturated Fat: 16.3
- Sugar: 44.2

95. Lemon Sour Cream Pound Cake

Serving: 1 10-inch cake, 10 serving(s) | Prep: 15mins | Ready in:

Ingredients

- 3 cups sugar
- 3 cups all-purpose flour
- 1⁄4 teaspoon salt
- 1⁄4 teaspoon baking soda
- 1 cup butter, softened
- 1 (8 ounce) container sour cream
- 6 large eggs
- 2 tablespoons lemon juice
- 1⁄2 teaspoon vanilla extract
- Lemon Glaze
- 1 cup powdered sugar
- 2 tablespoons fresh lemon juice
- 1⁄2 teaspoon vanilla extract
- 1 teaspoon grated lemon rind (optional)

Direction

- Place first 9 ingredients in a 4-qt mixing bowl (in that order). Beat at low speed with a heavy-duty mixer 1 minute, stopping to scrape down sides. Beat at medium speed 2 minutes. Spoon batter into a greased and floured 10-inch tube pan.
- Bake at 325°F for 1 hour and 30 minutes or until a wooden pick inserted in centre comes out clean. Cool cake in pan on a wire rack for 10 minutes; remove from pan, and cool on wire rack.
- Drizzle evenly with Lemon Glaze.
- Lemon Glaze: Stir together first 3 ingredients and, if desired, lemon rind until glaze is smooth. Makes about 1/3 cup.

Nutrition Information

- Calories: 669.7
- Fiber: 1
- Total Carbohydrate: 102
- Cholesterol: 172.8
- Total Fat: 26.4
- Saturated Fat: 15.4
- Sodium: 315.1
- Sugar: 72.9
- Protein: 8.3

96. Lemon Supreme Pound Cake

Serving: 2 loaves | Prep: 10mins | Ready in:

Ingredients

- 1 package lemon cake mix
- 1 (3 1/2 ounce) package instant lemon pudding
- 4 eggs
- 1 cup water
- 1⁄3 cup oil
- Glaze
- 1 cup icing sugar
- 1 tablespoon lemon juice
- 1 teaspoon grated fresh lemon rind

Direction

- In bowl, beat together cake mix, pudding mix, eggs, water and oil with mixer until smooth.
- Pour evenly into 2 greased loaf pans.
- Bake for 50-60 minutes at 350 or until done.
- Cool completely.
- For glaze combine ingredients in small bowl until well blended, spoon over loaves.
- This is good without the glaze also.

Nutrition Information

- Calories: 2019.1
- Total Carbohydrate: 312.3
- Saturated Fat: 12.4
- Sodium: 2511.4
- Fiber: 3
- Sugar: 173.3
- Cholesterol: 428.2
- Protein: 24.1
- Total Fat: 77

97. Lemon Glazed Mini Pound Cakes

Serving: 18 cakes | Prep: 20mins | Ready in:

Ingredients

- 3 large eggs
- 4 cups powdered sugar
- 1 1/4 cups unsalted butter, melted
- 2 1/2 cups all-purpose flour
- 1 teaspoon baking powder
- 1/4 teaspoon salt
- 3/4 cup milk
- 1/2 cup fresh lemon juice

Direction

- Preheat oven to 350 degrees.
- Spray 18 muffin cups with cooking spray. In a large bowl, using a handheld mixer, beat the eggs at low speed until blended. Add 3 cups of the sugar, melted butter, flour, baking powder, and salt. Beat at medium speed until smooth, about 1 minute. Beat in the milk.
- Spoon 1/4 cup batter into each prepared muffin cup. Bake for 25 minutes, until golden and a toothpick inserted in the middle comes out clean. Let cool for 5 minutes, then turn cakes out onto a rack to cool for 30 minutes.
- In a saucepan, whisk the remaining 1 cup of sugar with the lemon juice and bring to a simmer over moderate heat, stirring, until thickened to a syrup, 8 minutes. Let cool.
- Brush the tops of the pound cakes with the lemon syrup. Let stand until the glaze has set, 10 minutes. Brush again with the remaining syrup, let set. Serve.

Nutrition Information

- Calories: 300.5
- Sodium: 71.5
- Fiber: 0.5
- Total Fat: 14.2
- Saturated Fat: 8.6
- Sugar: 26.4
- Total Carbohydrate: 41
- Cholesterol: 70.6
- Protein: 3.3

98. Lemon Poppy Seed Pound Cake

Serving: 1 9x5inch loaf, 8 serving(s) | Prep: 10mins | Ready in:

Ingredients

- 1 cup unsalted butter
- 1 1/2 cups cake flour
- 1 teaspoon baking powder
- 1/2 teaspoon salt
- 1/3 cup poppy seed
- 1 1/4 cups sugar
- 2 tablespoons grated lemons, zest of
- 2 teaspoons fresh lemon juice
- 4 large eggs
- 1 1/2 teaspoons vanilla extract
- For Glaze
- 1/2 cup sugar
- 1/4 cup lemon juice

Direction

- Preheat oven to 350°F.
- Grease 9x5-inch loaf pan with softened butter and dust with flour.
- In medium bowl, whisk together flour, baking powder, and salt; set aside.
- Take 1 tablespoon of flour mixture and toss with poppy seeds in a small bowl, set aside.
- Melt butter (I use microwave--but be sure not to leave it in too long or it will bubble over).
- In food processor, process sugar and zest until combined--just a few short pulses.
- Add lemon juice, eggs and vanilla; process until combined, about 5 seconds.

- With machine running, add melted butter through feed tube (this should take about 20 seconds).
- Transfer mixture to large bowl.
- Sift flour mixture over eggs in thirds, whisking gently after each addition until just combined.
- Gently fold in poppy seeds until evenly incorporated.
- Pour batter into prepared pan and bake 15 minutes.
- Reduce oven temperature to 325°F and continue baking until deep golden brown and skewer inserted in center comes out clean (about 35 minutes).
- Cool in pan for 10 minutes, then turn onto a wire rack and brush on Lemon Glaze, if desired.
- Cool to room temperature.
- For glaze: While loaf is cooling, bring sugar and lemon juice to a boil in a small nonreactive saucepan, stirring occasionally to dissolve sugar.
- Reduce heat to low and simmer until thickened slightly, about 2 minutes.
- After removing cake from pan, poke entire top and sides with a toothpick.
- Brush top and sides of cake with glaze.
- I like to do this while cake is on cooling rack over sink or waxed paper as it can be messy!

Nutrition Information

- Calories: 538.5
- Saturated Fat: 15.7
- Cholesterol: 166.8
- Protein: 6.6
- Total Fat: 28.3
- Fiber: 1.1
- Sugar: 45.1
- Total Carbohydrate: 66.4
- Sodium: 230.8

99. Lottie's Lemon Pound Cake

Serving: 2 Loaves | Prep: 30mins | Ready in:

Ingredients

- 1 cup butter or 1 cup Crisco
- 2 cups sugar
- 4 eggs
- 1 tablespoon lemon extract
- 1/2 teaspoon vanilla
- 1 tablespoon white wine
- 1/2 teaspoon salt
- 3 cups sifted all-purpose flour
- 3/4 cup buttermilk
- 1 teaspoon baking soda
- 1 tablespoon white vinegar

Direction

- Preheat oven to 325°F.
- In a large bowl, cream butter (or Crisco) and sugar together.
- Beat in eggs, one at a time.
- Add lemon extract, vanilla, wine and salt, stir to mix well.
- Sift flour and add it alternately with the buttermilk to the butter mixture.
- Mix baking soda and vinegar together, and stir into batter.
- Stir batter to mix all ingredients well.
- Grease and flour 2 (8 x 4-inch) loaf pans.
- Divide batter evenly into both pans.
- Bake at 325°F for about 60-70 minutes, or until a toothpick inserted into the center of the loaf comes out clean.
- Remove from oven, and cool on wire racks.

Nutrition Information

- Calories: 2475.9
- Total Fat: 104.2
- Saturated Fat: 62.2
- Sugar: 205.2
- Sodium: 2266.3
- Fiber: 5.1
- Total Carbohydrate: 348.8

- Cholesterol: 619.7
- Protein: 35.9

- Sodium: 136
- Sugar: 12.7
- Total Carbohydrate: 23.2
- Cholesterol: 73.2

100. Makeover Pound Cake

Serving: 1 loaf, 12 serving(s) | Prep: 15mins | Ready in:

Ingredients

- 1/2 cup butter, softened
- 3/4 cup sugar
- 3 eggs
- 1/4 cup unsweetened applesauce
- 1 1/4 teaspoons vanilla extract
- 1/2 teaspoon grated lemon peel
- 1 1/4 cups all-purpose flour
- 1/2 teaspoon baking powder
- 1/4 teaspoon salt

Direction

- In a small mixing bowl, cream butter and sugar until light and fluffy, about 5 minutes.
- Add eggs, one at a time, beating well after each egg addition.
- Stir in the applesauce, vanilla and lemon peel.
- Combine the flour, baking powder and salt together and add to the creamed mixture just until blended.
- Transfer to an 8" loaf pan which has been sprayed with non-stick cooking spray.
- Bake at 350F for 45-55 minutes or until golden brown and cake tester inserted comes out clean.
- Cool for 10 minutes before removing to a wire rack to cool completely.

Nutrition Information

- Calories: 185.5
- Saturated Fat: 5.3
- Fiber: 0.4
- Protein: 3
- Total Fat: 9

101. Maple Grilled Pound Cake With Peaches

Serving: 8 serving(s) | Prep: 15mins | Ready in:

Ingredients

- 16 peeled peach halves in syrup (fresh or canned)
- 1/4 cup orange juice
- 2 tablespoons butter, melted
- 2 tablespoons pure maple syrup, plus more for serving
- 1 loaf poundcake, cut into 1 inch slices (8-inch)

Direction

- Prepare a medium fire in the grill.
- Combine the orange juice, butter and maple syrup.
- Brush onto the peaches and both sides of the cake slices.
- Grill peaches and cake slices until golden brown, about 5 minutes per side for the peaches, 3 minutes per side for the cake.
- Place a slice of cake and 2 peach halves on each plate.
- Drizzle with maple syrup if desired.
- Serve at once.

Nutrition Information

- Calories: 332.5
- Saturated Fat: 6.2
- Sugar: 40.2
- Protein: 3
- Cholesterol: 90.5
- Total Fat: 10.6
- Sodium: 182

- Fiber: 2.8
- Total Carbohydrate: 61.5

102. Marvelous Maraschino Mini Pound Cakes

Serving: 6 mini loaves | Prep: 25mins | Ready in:

Ingredients

- 1 1/4 cups butter, softened
- 2 3/4 cups sugar
- 5 large eggs, at room temperature
- 1 teaspoon vanilla extract
- 3 cups flour
- 1 teaspoon baking powder
- 1/4 teaspoon salt
- 1 (14 ounce) can sweetened condensed milk
- 2 cups quartered maraschino cherries, well drained
- powdered sugar, for dusting

Direction

- Preheat oven to 350*F. Grease and flour six 6x3" loaf pans.
- In a large bowl, using an electric mixer, cream together the butter, sugar, eggs, and vanilla on low speed until blended, then on high speed for 5 minutes until light and fluffy.
- In another bowl, whisk together the flour, baking powder, and salt.
- Add the flour mixture to the butter mixture alternately with the condensed milk, blending lightly after each addition. Fold in the cherries.
- Divide batter evenly among the prepared pans; bake for 45 minutes or until a toothpick tests done.
- Cool in pans for 5 minutes; remove from pans and cool completely on wire racks. Dust with powdered sugar.

Nutrition Information

- Calories: 1197.3
- Cholesterol: 300.4
- Protein: 17.3
- Saturated Fat: 29.3
- Sodium: 573.5
- Total Carbohydrate: 175.9
- Sugar: 128.2
- Total Fat: 48.9
- Fiber: 1.7

103. Mascarpone Cheese Pound Cake

Serving: 6-8 slice pound cake, 6-8 serving(s) | Prep: 15mins | Ready in:

Ingredients

- 1 cup butter, room temperature
- 1/2 cup shortening
- 3 cups granulated sugar
- 1 (16 ounce) container mascarpone cheese or 1 (8 ounce) package cream cheese, room temperature
- 3 cups all-purpose flour, sifted before measuring
- 6 eggs
- 1 tablespoon vanilla extract
- 1 pint raspberries
- 1 quart strawberry
- 1 pint blueberries
- 1 pint blackberry
- 1 cup sugar
- 1 cup orange liqueur
- 1 bunch of fresh mint
- 1 lb cake
- whipped cream, for garnish
- fresh mint sprig, for garnish

Direction

- In a large mixing bowl, cream butter and shortening. With electric hand-held mixer on medium speed, gradually beat in the sugar.

Beat in mascarpone cheese. Add flour, alternating with the eggs, beginning and ending with flour. Stir in vanilla. Pour batter into a greased and floured 10-inch tube pan or Bundt cake pan. Bake at 325° for about 1 hour and 15 minutes or until a wooden pick comes out clean when inserted in the center. Let cool in pan for 10 minutes, then remove to a rack to cool completely.

- For Berry Salad:
- In a large bowl, add all berries and sugar.
- Mash berries slightly and add orange liqueur. Let sit for 30 minutes until ready to serve.
- Slice pound cake and top with macerated berries and whipped cream. Garnish with mint.

Nutrition Information

- Calories: 1351.8
- Total Fat: 54.2
- Fiber: 10.8
- Cholesterol: 267.3
- Saturated Fat: 25.4
- Sodium: 346.4
- Sugar: 148.2
- Total Carbohydrate: 207.4
- Protein: 15.4

---

104.   Mexican Chocolate Pound Cake

Serving: 1 bundt pan | Prep: 20mins | Ready in:

Ingredients

- 3 1/2 cups flour
- 1 cup unsweetened cocoa powder (use Mexican for authenticity!)
- 2 teaspoons ground cinnamon
- 2 teaspoons baking powder
- 1/2 teaspoon salt
- 1 lb unsalted butter, at room temp
- 2 cups light brown sugar

- 1 cup sugar
- 6 eggs, at room temp
- 1/2 cup whole milk, at room temp
- 1/2 cup strong coffee, at room temp
- 1 teaspoon vanilla

Direction

- Preheat oven to 350°.
- Generously grease and flour pans (see description above).
- Sift the flour, cocoa powder, cinnamon, baking powder and salt into a bowl.
- Place the butter and sugars in mixer bowl, fitted with paddle if possible, and beat until smooth and creamy.
- Add eggs, one at a time, beating well and scraping down sides of bowl before each addition.
- Add half the flour mixture and beat well, then add the milk, coffee and vanilla.
- Scrape down sides and add remaining flour mixture. Beat well.
- Pour batter into prepared pan(s). Transfer to oven and bake until cake pulls away from the sides, and tester comes out NOT QUITE clean, about 50-55 minutes for Bundt pan, 45 minutes for 9x5, and 40 minutes for 8x4's. These times are not exact -- they may take up to 15 minutes longer!
- Cool for 20 minutes in pan, then invert on rack. Cool to room temperature.

Nutrition Information

- Calories: 8024.1
- Saturated Fat: 252.5
- Sodium: 2572.6
- Protein: 108.3
- Total Carbohydrate: 1030.5
- Cholesterol: 2104.3
- Total Fat: 416.9
- Fiber: 43.2
- Sugar: 637.4

105. Milk Chocolate Pound Cake

Serving: 12-14 serving(s) | Prep: 20mins | Ready in:

Ingredients

- 4 (1 5/8 ounce) milk chocolate candy bars
- 1 yellow cake mix
- 1 (3 1/2 ounce) vanilla instant pudding mix
- 1 cup sour cream
- 1/2 cup vegetable oil
- 4 large eggs
- 1 teaspoon vanilla extract
- 2 teaspoons powdered sugar

Direction

- Preheat oven to 350 degrees.
- Spray a 12 cup Bundt pan or a tube pan with non-stick spray containing flour (Baker's Joy or Crisco with flour)
- Break milk chocolate bars into pieces.
- Chop chocolate pieces into small bits - some may be large.
- Combine cake mix, pudding mix, sour cream, oil, eggs, and vanilla in a large bowl.
- Beat with mixer on low speed for 1 minute. Fold in chocolate bits.
- Pour batter into prepared pan.
- Smooth out with spatula.
- Bake in pre-heated 350 degree oven for 55 to 60 minutes or until cake is lightly browned and cake springs back when lightly pressed. Allow cake to cool 20 minutes.
- Place cake on a serving platter and sift powdered sugar over the top.

Nutrition Information

- Calories: 446.4
- Protein: 5.8
- Total Fat: 24.2
- Saturated Fat: 7.1
- Sodium: 447.7
- Fiber: 1
- Sugar: 34.6
- Total Carbohydrate: 51.7
- Cholesterol: 83.2

106. Mini Morsel Chocolate Chip Pound Cake

Serving: 1 cake, 12 serving(s) | Prep: 10mins | Ready in:

Ingredients

- 1 cup butter, softened
- 2 cups sugar
- 3 cups all-purpose flour
- 1 teaspoon baking powder
- 1/2 teaspoon salt
- 3 teaspoons vanilla extract
- 4 eggs
- 3/4 cup milk
- 2 cups mini morsel chocolate chips (1 bag)
- confectioners' sugar, for dusting

Direction

- Preheat oven to 350 degrees.
- Grease and flour a 10 inches tube/Bundt pan or 1-2 loaf pans.
- In a small bowl, combine the flour, baking powder and salt. Set aside.
- In mixer, beat the sugar and butter until creamy, then add the vanilla.
- Beat in eggs, one at a time, until each one is incorporated.
- Gradually mix in the flour mixture, alternating with milk.
- Stir in the chocolate chips.
- Pour into floured pan/pans.
- Bake 70-80 minute or until toothpick, when inserted, comes out clean.
- Cool 10 min., loosen sides and invert onto cake plate, cover with lid until cake is room temperature. (This will make for a moist cake).

When there is no more moisture on top of cake, dust it with the confectioner sugar.

Nutrition Information

- Calories: 549.6
- Fiber: 2.5
- Sugar: 48.8
- Total Carbohydrate: 76.1
- Cholesterol: 104.8
- Protein: 7.2
- Total Fat: 26.2
- Saturated Fat: 15.6
- Sodium: 297.5

107. Mini Pumpkin Pound Cakes

Serving: 4 mini loaf cakes | Prep: 25mins | Ready in:

Ingredients

- 2 1/2 cups sugar
- 3/4 cup butter, melted
- 1/4 cup vegetable oil
- 3 large eggs
- 3 cups flour
- 2 teaspoons baking soda
- 1 teaspoon cinnamon
- 1 teaspoon nutmeg
- 1/4 teaspoon clove
- 1/2 teaspoon salt
- 1 (15 ounce) can solid-pack pumpkin

Direction

- Set oven to 350 degrees, (second lowest position).
- Grease bottoms only of mini loaf pans.
- In a large bowl, beat together sugar, butter, oil; add eggs, until well combined (about 2-3 minutes).
- Combine/sift flour, baking soda, cinnamon, nutmeg, cloves and salt.

- Add the dry mixture to egg mixture, with canned pumpkin; mix well.
- Pour/transfer into regular or fluted mini loaf pans, filling 3/4 full.
- Bake for about 25-30 minutes, or until cake test done with toothpick.

Nutrition Information

- Calories: 1338.6
- Total Fat: 53.2
- Sugar: 127.1
- Total Carbohydrate: 204.6
- Cholesterol: 250.1
- Protein: 15.9
- Saturated Fat: 25.1
- Sodium: 1221.2
- Fiber: 3.5

108. Mississippi Cream Cheese Pound Cake

Serving: 16 serving(s) | Prep: 20mins | Ready in:

Ingredients

- 1 1/2 cups butter
- 1 (8 ounce) package cream cheese, softened
- 3 cups sugar
- 6 eggs
- 1 egg yolk
- 2 teaspoons vanilla extract
- 3 cups cake flour

Direction

- Preheat oven to 325°F Grease and flour a 12-cup Bundt pan, tube pan or two 9-by-5-inch loaf pans.
- Combine butter, cream cheese, sugar, eggs and egg yolk, and vanilla in large bowl; beat until smooth.
- Add cake flour ½ cup at a time. Stir together until smooth.

- Pour into pan. Bake 70 minutes or until a toothpick inserted in the center comes out clean. Serves 16.

Nutrition Information

- Calories: 470.7
- Total Fat: 24.4
- Total Carbohydrate: 58.4
- Cholesterol: 141.5
- Protein: 5.6
- Saturated Fat: 14.4
- Sodium: 225.6
- Fiber: 0.4
- Sugar: 38.1

109.   Moist, Dense, Heavy Cream Pound Cake

Serving: 2 loafs, 10 serving(s) | Prep: 15mins | Ready in:

Ingredients

- 3 cups granulated sugar
- 1 cup butter, softened (two sticks, no substitutions!)
- 7 large eggs
- 3 cups cake flour
- 1 cup heavy whipping cream
- 2 teaspoons vanilla extract
- OPTIONAL
- 1 teaspoon maple extract (optional) or 1 teaspoon butter flavor extract (optional) or 1 teaspoon almond extract (optional) or 2 teaspoons lemon juice (optional) or 2 teaspoons orange juice (optional)

Direction

- Cream sugar and softened butter until smooth.
- Add eggs in 1 at a time, mixing well between each addition.
- Sift in 1 1/2 cups cake flour, and combine.
- Add heavy cream to mixture, stir in well.

- Sift in the remaining 1 1/2 cups cake flour and combine until smooth.
- Stir in vanilla extract and additional optional flavors.
- Pour into Greased and floured Bundt pan or 2 loaf pans.
- Place in the middle of a cold oven, turn on heat to 350 degrees F.
- Bake 60-70 minutes, until a knife inserted in the middle of the cake comes out clean.
- (The smaller the pan, the less time it will take to bake.).
- Remove from oven and let cool before removing from pan.
- Store in an airtight container or wrap with aluminum foil.

Nutrition Information

- Calories: 679.7
- Sodium: 189.7
- Fiber: 0.7
- Total Carbohydrate: 93.1
- Total Fat: 31.1
- Saturated Fat: 18.3
- Sugar: 60.5
- Cholesterol: 229.5
- Protein: 8.4

110.   Moroccan Pound Cake

Serving: 12 serving(s) | Prep: 15mins | Ready in:

Ingredients

- 2/3 cup oleo
- 1/2 cup vegetable shortening
- 2 cups sugar
- 4 eggs
- 3 cups all-purpose flour
- 3 teaspoons baking powder
- 1/4 teaspoon salt
- 1 cup milk
- 1 teaspoon vanilla

- 1/2 cup raisins
- 3/4 cup nuts, chopped, unsalted, mixed
- 1 tablespoon cocoa
- 1 tablespoon cinnamon

Direction

- Preheat oven to 350°.
- Cream margarine and sugar until light.
- Add eggs, one at a time, beating thoroughly after each.
- Add sifted dry ingredients alternately with milk, beating until smooth.
- Add vanilla, raisins and nuts. Pour 3/4 of batter into a 10-inch tube pan lined on bottom with waxed paper.
- Mix remaining batter with cocoa and cinnamon and spoon onto batter in pan. Run a knife through batter to marbleize.
- Bake at 350° about 1 hour and 15 minutes.
- Let stand in pan 5 minutes, then turn out on rack; peel off paper. Cool and sprinkle with powdered sugar.

Nutrition Information

- Calories: 519.6
- Total Carbohydrate: 66.3
- Protein: 7.9
- Saturated Fat: 6
- Sodium: 349.5
- Fiber: 2.2
- Sugar: 37.5
- Cholesterol: 73.3
- Total Fat: 25.8

111.   My Favorite Pound Cake

Serving: 1 cake, 10 serving(s) | Prep: 15mins | Ready in:

Ingredients

- 1 cup unsalted butter, room temperature
- 1/2 cup shortening

- 3 cups cake flour, preferably Soft As Silk brand
- 3 cups sugar
- 5 eggs
- 1 cup whole milk
- 1 teaspoon baking powder
- 1 teaspoon vanilla
- 1 teaspoon lemon extract

Direction

- Cream butter, shortening and sugar until light and fluffy.
- Add eggs one at a time, beating well after each addition.
- Sift dry ingredients together.
- Add vanilla and lemon extract to milk.
- Add dry ingredients to sugar and egg mixture, alternating with liquid, beating just to blend, until all ingredients are combined.
- Beat batter on medium speed for 5 minutes.
- Place into greased and floured 10-inch tube pan and place into COLD oven.
- Bake at 350 degrees for 1 hour and 15-20 minutes until a cake tester inserted in the middle comes out clean.

Nutrition Information

- Calories: 688.1
- Sodium: 84.4
- Fiber: 0.7
- Sugar: 61.6
- Protein: 7.5
- Total Fat: 32.3
- Saturated Fat: 15.5
- Total Carbohydrate: 93.5
- Cholesterol: 157

112.   My Favorite Sour Cream Pound Cake

Serving: 12 serving(s) | Prep: 20mins | Ready in:

Ingredients

- 1 cup butter, softened
- 3 cups sugar
- 6 eggs, separated
- 2 cups all-purpose flour
- 1 cup self-rising flour
- 1 cup sour cream

Direction

- Cream butter and sugar together.
- Add the egg yolks.
- Sift the flours together and add with sour cream to mixture.
- Beat egg whites till stiff and add to mixture.
- Bake in a buttered and floured tube pan at 325F for approximately one hour and thirty minutes or until done.

Nutrition Information

- Calories: 519.6
- Protein: 7.1
- Saturated Fat: 13
- Fiber: 0.8
- Sugar: 50.3
- Total Carbohydrate: 74.6
- Cholesterol: 154.8
- Total Fat: 22.1
- Sodium: 286.8

---

113. My Mom's Pound Cake

Serving: 1 serving(s) | Prep: 20mins | Ready in:

Ingredients

- 1 1/2 cups margarine or 1 1/2 cups butter
- 3 cups sugar
- 5 eggs
- 3 cups flour
- 1 cup milk
- 1 teaspoon vanilla extract
- 1 teaspoon lemon extract
- 1 teaspoon orange extract

- 1/4 teaspoon mace (optional)
- 1/2 teaspoon baking powder

Direction

- Cream butter and sugar in mixer until well blended.
- Add eggs, one at a time and beat well.
- Add flour, alternating with the milk.
- Start with the flour and end with the flour.
- Lastly, add flavorings and baking powder by hand.
- (I found that the mace, although expensive adds to the taste).
- Bake in tube pan, greased and floured in 325 degree oven for 1 hour and 15 minutes.
- When cool, wrap in Reynolds Wrap.

Nutrition Information

- Calories: 6679.1
- Saturated Fat: 61.3
- Sodium: 3850.6
- Fiber: 10.1
- Total Carbohydrate: 904.1
- Total Fat: 309.9
- Protein: 81.2
- Sugar: 603.5
- Cholesterol: 1091.7

---

114. Never Fail Pound Cake Paula Deen

Serving: 1 10-inch bundt pan, 10-12 serving(s) | Prep: 10mins | Ready in:

Ingredients

- 1/2 cup butter, softened
- 3 cups sugar
- 5 eggs
- 3 cups cake flour
- 1 cup milk
- 2 teaspoons lemon extract

- vanilla ice cream
- berries, for garnish

Direction

- Special equipment: a 10-inch Bundt pan, greased and floured
- In a large bowl, using a mixer, combine the butter and sugar until creamy.
- Add the eggs, 1 at a time, beating well after each addition.
- Add the flour and milk alternately, beginning and ending with the flour.
- Stir in the lemon extract.
- Spoon the batter into the prepared pan.
- Place pan in a cold oven and heat oven to 325 degrees F. Bake cake for 1 hour. Increase the temperature to 350 degrees F and bake for 30 minutes more.
- *Cook's Note: Do not open the oven door while baking.
- Cool the cake in the pan for 10 minutes, and then turn out onto a wire rack to cool.

Nutrition Information

- Calories: 515.7
- Total Fat: 12.8
- Saturated Fat: 7.2
- Sodium: 129.9
- Sugar: 60.1
- Fiber: 0.7
- Total Carbohydrate: 93.4
- Cholesterol: 120.8
- Protein: 7.4

115.   Nuts Stuff Pound Cake

Serving: 1 bunt cake, 12 serving(s) | Prep: 10mins | Ready in:

Ingredients

- 1 (18 ounce) yellow cake mix (or white)

- 1 (3 1/2 ounce) package vanilla instant pudding mix
- 1 (8 ounce) carton sour cream
- 4 eggs
- 1/2 cup vegetable oil
- 1/2 cup sugar
- 1/2 cup chopped nuts
- 2 tablespoons cinnamon

Direction

- Mix first 5 ingredients for about 7 minute.
- In separate bowl mix the last ingredients.
- Grease a bunt cake pan.
- Pour 1/2 of the batter in the pan.
- Sprinkle with 1/2 of the sugar mixture.
- Repeat layers.
- Lightly press topping into the batter with the back of a spoon.
- Bake at 350 for 50-55 minute.

Nutrition Information

- Calories: 431.4
- Sugar: 34.9
- Total Carbohydrate: 52.5
- Total Fat: 22.9
- Saturated Fat: 5.5
- Sodium: 470.8
- Fiber: 1.6
- Cholesterol: 80.1
- Protein: 5.6

116.   Old Fashioned Pound Cake 1972

Serving: 1 loaf pan size cake, 10 serving(s) | Prep: 10mins | Ready in:

Ingredients

- 1 2/3 cups white sugar
- 1 cup soft butter

- 2 cups cake flour or 1 3/4 cups all-purpose flour, sifted then measured
- 1/2 teaspoon salt
- 1/4 teaspoon ground mace
- 5 whole eggs
- 1 teaspoon vanilla

Direction

- Pre heat oven to 325 degrees.
- Grease loaf pan. Can line if desired.
- Cream butter and sugar until all granules are dissolved and you no longer feel them between your fingertips.
- Sift the flour and measure.
- Add the salt and mace.
- Sift all together once more.
- Add eggs one at a time, alternating with the flour to the creamed mixture.
- Beat until light and fluffy.
- Add the vanilla.
- Pour into prepared greased pan.
- Bake 325 degrees for 50 to 60 minutes.
- Using tester to test.

Nutrition Information

- Calories: 424.7
- Sugar: 33.6
- Total Carbohydrate: 55
- Cholesterol: 141.9
- Protein: 5.2
- Total Fat: 20.9
- Saturated Fat: 12.4
- Sodium: 278.4
- Fiber: 0.5

---

117.   One Step Pound Cake 1969

Serving: 18 serving(s) | Prep: 10mins | Ready in:

Ingredients

- 2 1/4 cups all-purpose flour
- 2 cups granulated sugar
- 1/2 teaspoon salt
- 1/2 teaspoon baking soda
- 1 teaspoon grated fresh lemon rind (optional)
- 1 teaspoon vanilla
- 1 cup soft room temp butter
- 1 cup sour cream (or pineapple yogurt)
- 3 whole eggs

Direction

- Place all in a large mixer bowl. Blend on low speed. Beat at med. speed for 4 minutes. Pour into a greased and floured Bundt or tube pan.
- Bake 325 degrees F for 60 - 70 minutes.
- Until golden and cake springs back when tested.
- Cool upright in the pan for 20 minutes.
- Remove from pan, cool completely.
- Glaze when cool.
- Glaze: 1 cup powdered icing sugar with 2 tbsp. lemon juice.

Nutrition Information

- Calories: 272.1
- Total Fat: 13.8
- Saturated Fat: 8.4
- Sugar: 22.4
- Total Carbohydrate: 34.8
- Protein: 3
- Sodium: 189.6
- Fiber: 0.4
- Cholesterol: 63.8

---

118.   Orange Cranberry Pound Cake

Serving: 10-14 serving(s) | Prep: 20mins | Ready in:

Ingredients

- 1 1/4 cups butter, at room temperature

- 1 (8 ounce) package cream cheese, room temperature
- 2 cups sugar
- 6 eggs
- 1/2 teaspoon vanilla
- 2 oranges, zest of, grated
- 4 cups all-purpose flour
- 2 teaspoons baking powder
- 1/2 teaspoon clove
- 1/4 teaspoon salt
- 2 1/4 cups fresh cranberries, chopped

Direction

- Preheat oven to 350 degrees.
- Grease and flour 9 inch Bundt pan.
- In mixing bowl, using mixer on medium speed, cream butter, cream cheese, and sugar until light and fluffy.
- Reduce speed to low and mix in eggs one at a time.
- Add vanilla and orange zest, scraping the sides of the bowl after each addition.
- Stir together dry ingredients (flour, baking powder, cloves, and salt) in a medium bowl, mixing well.
- Gradually add the dry ingredients to the butter mixture.
- Beat on low speed until smooth.
- DO NOT over beat.
- Fold in cranberries.
- Pour into the nonstick prepared Bundt cake pan (I do spray mine lightly with PAM to prevent sticking).
- Bake for 50 to 55 minutes or until knife inserted in the center comes out clean.
- Cool completely before serving and dust with powdered sugar if desired.

Nutrition Information

- Calories: 674.8
- Total Fat: 34.5
- Saturated Fat: 20.6
- Sugar: 41.3
- Cholesterol: 212.8

- Sodium: 405
- Fiber: 2.4
- Total Carbohydrate: 81.9
- Protein: 11

119.   Orange Glazed Pound Cake

Serving: 12 serving(s) | Prep: 15mins | Ready in:

Ingredients

- 1 (18 1/4 ounce) package butter recipe cake mix
- 4 eggs
- 1 cup sour cream
- 1/3 cup vegetable oil
- 1/4 cup orange juice
- 1 -2 tablespoon orange juice
- 2 tablespoons grated orange peel
- 1 cup confectioners' sugar

Direction

- Preheat oven to 375 degrees.
- Grease and flour a 10 inch tube pan.
- Combine cake mix, eggs, sour cream, oil, 1/4 cup orange juice and orange peel in large bowl. Beat at medium speed with electric mixer for 2 minutes. Pour into prepared pan. Bake at 375 degrees for 45 minutes or until a toothpick inserted near center comes out clean. Cool in pan for 25 minutes. Invert onto cooling rack. Cool completely.
- Combine sugar and remaining 1 to 2 tablespoons orange juice in small bowl. Stir until smooth. Drizzle over cake.

Nutrition Information

- Calories: 348
- Fiber: 0.6
- Total Carbohydrate: 45.5
- Cholesterol: 79.8

- Sodium: 317
- Sugar: 29.2
- Protein: 4.7
- Total Fat: 16.8
- Saturated Fat: 4.5

120. Orange Poppy Seed Pound Cake (Lighten Up Recipe)

Serving: 12 serving(s) | Prep: 20mins | Ready in:

Ingredients

- 1 3/4 cups all-purpose flour
- 1/2 teaspoon baking powder
- 1/2 teaspoon baking soda
- 1/2 teaspoon salt
- 2/3 cup granulated sugar
- 1/3 cup oil
- 3 egg whites
- 1 tablespoon poppy seed
- 2 teaspoons grated orange zest
- 3/4 cup low-fat milk
- 2 teaspoons low-fat milk
- 1/2 cup confectioners' sugar
- orange zest, strips (for garnish) (optional)

Direction

- Preheat oven to 350 degrees F.
- Grease and flour 8 1/2 x 4 1/2 x 2 1/2" loaf pan.
- Combine flour, baking powder, soda and salt; reserve.
- On medium speed beat granulated sugar, oil and egg whites until blended. On low, beat in poppy seeds, 1 1/2 t zest and flour mixture.
- Beat in 3/4 c milk until smooth.
- Pour batter into pan.
- Bake 50 minutes or until toothpick inserted into center comes out clean.
- Cool 10 minutes. Remove from pan; cool completely on rack.

- Whisk confectioners' sugar with remaining 2 t of milk and 1/2 t zest; pour over cake.
- Garnish with orange zest strips, if desired.

Nutrition Information

- Calories: 197.7
- Total Fat: 6.7
- Sodium: 185.8
- Fiber: 0.6
- Sugar: 17.1
- Protein: 3.5
- Saturated Fat: 1.1
- Total Carbohydrate: 31.2
- Cholesterol: 0.8

121. Orange Pound Cake With Orange Caramel Sauce

Serving: 12 serving(s) | Prep: 20mins | Ready in:

Ingredients

- 1 1/2 cups all-purpose flour
- 1/2 teaspoon salt
- 1/4 teaspoon baking powder
- 1/4 teaspoon baking soda
- 1 large orange
- 1 cup sugar
- 1/2 cup buttermilk, at room temperature
- 1/2 teaspoon vanilla extract
- 1/4 cup butter, softened (no substitutions)
- 1 large egg
- 2 large egg whites
- Orange/Caramel Sauce
- 2 tablespoons water
- 1/4 cup sugar

Direction

- Preheat oven to 350*F degrees.
- Lightly coat a 9x5-inch loaf pan with vegetable cooking spray.

- Sift together flour, salt, baking powder and baking soda in medium bowl; set aside.
- With vegetable peeler remove peel from orange; coarsely chop.
- Cut orange in half and squeeze 1/2 cup juice.
- Process sugar and peel in food processor, pulsing until peel is finely chopped.
- Combine buttermilk, 1/4 cup orange juice and vanilla in a small glass measuring cup (Reserve remaining juice for caramel sauce).
- Beat butter and orange-sugar mixture in large mixer bowl on medium-high speed until combined.
- Beat in egg and egg whites, one at a time, beating well after each addition.
- At low speed, add flour mixture alternately with buttermilk mixture, beginning and ending with dry ingredients.
- Spoon batter into prepared pan.
- Bake 35 to 40 minutes or until toothpick inserted in center comes out clean.
- Cool on wire rack 15 minutes; invert and remove pan.
- Make Orange-Caramel Sauce: Meanwhile, combine water and sugar in small saucepan; stir with wooden spoon until sugar is moistened.
- Bring to simmer over medium-low heat; cover and simmer 2 to 3 minutes until sugar dissolves.
- Uncover and cook until sugar turns amber, 5 to 6 minutes.
- Remove from heat and slowly stir in reserved orange juice (mixture will bubble vigorously).
- Return to heat and cook, stirring, until sugar dissolves.
- Cool sauce and serve with cake.

Nutrition Information

- Calories: 192.1
- Protein: 3.3
- Saturated Fat: 2.6
- Sodium: 190.8
- Fiber: 0.8
- Sugar: 22.8

- Total Fat: 4.5
- Total Carbohydrate: 35.2
- Cholesterol: 26.1

122. Orange Coconut Pound Cake

Serving: 16 serving(s) | Prep: 30mins | Ready in:

Ingredients

- Cake
- 1 1/2 cups butter, at room temperature
- 2 1/2 cups sugar
- 5 eggs, at room temperature
- 3 1/2 cups flour
- 1/2 teaspoon baking powder
- 1/2 teaspoon salt
- 1/2 cup Coco Lopez
- 3/4 cup orange juice
- 1 teaspoon orange extract
- 1 teaspoon vanilla extract
- 1 tablespoon grated orange peel
- Glaze
- 1 cup confectioners' sugar
- 1 tablespoon orange liqueur
- 2 tablespoons grated coconut
- 2 tablespoons unsalted butter
- 2 tablespoons orange juice
- 1 tablespoon Coco Lopez

Direction

- Preheat oven to 350°F.
- Grease and flour a large tube pan and line the bottom of the pan with greased waxed paper.
- Sift together the flour, baking powder and salt. Combine the cream of coconut and orange juice.
- With an electric mixer at medium speed, cream the butter until light and fluffy.
- While still beating, add the sugar a little at a time until all the sugar is incorporated into the mixture.

- Add eggs one at a time, beating well after each addition.
- Alternate adding the flour and liquid, beating after each addition.
- At low speed stir in the extracts and orange peel.
- Pour batter into the tube pan and bake for about 1 hour 15 minutes, or until a toothpick inserted near the center comes out clean.
- Make the glaze just before the cake comes out of the oven.
- Combine all glaze ingredients in a small saucepan.
- Cook over low heat until warmed through and butter is melted. Do not boil.
- Drizzle over warm cake.

Nutrition Information

- Calories: 472.8
- Total Fat: 23.1
- Fiber: 1.2
- Total Carbohydrate: 62.4
- Protein: 5.4
- Saturated Fat: 14.6
- Sodium: 235.1
- Sugar: 40.7
- Cholesterol: 115.7

123. Orange Pecan Spice Pound Cake

Serving: 1 10inch tube cake, 10-12 serving(s) | Prep: 25mins | Ready in:

Ingredients

- 2 cups finely chopped pecans, toasted and divided
- 1 lb butter, softened
- 3 cups sugar
- 6 large eggs
- 4 cups all-purpose flour
- 1/8 teaspoon salt
- 1/2 teaspoon baking powder
- 3/4 cup milk
- 2 tablespoons grated orange rind
- 2 teaspoons ground cinnamon
- 1 teaspoon ground nutmeg
- 1 teaspoon vanilla extract
- 1 teaspoon lemon extract
- 1 teaspoon orange extract
- 1/2 teaspoon ground cloves
- For Orange Syrup
- 1 large orange
- 1 cup sugar
- For Glazed Pecan Halves
- 1 cup pecan halves
- 3 tablespoons light corn syrup
- vegetable oil cooking spray

Direction

- Sprinkle 1 1/4 cups finely chopped pecans into a generously buttered 10-inch tube pan; shake to evenly coat bottom and sides of pan. (The food processor is great for chopping those nuts!)
- (Excess nuts will fall to bottom of pan. Make certain nuts are in an even layer in bottom of pan.) Set aside.
- Preheat oven to 300°F.
- Beat butter at medium speed with an electric mixer until creamy; gradually add sugar, beating well.
- Add eggs, 1 at a time; beating until blended after each addition.
- Combine flour, salt and baking powder; add to butter mixture alternately with milk, beginning and ending with flour mixture.
- Beat at low speed until blended after each addition.
- Stir in remaining 3/4 cup pecans, grated orange rind, cinnamon, nutmeg, and next 4 ingredients.
- Spoon batter evenly into prepared pan.
- Bake at 300°F for about 1 1/2 hours or until wooden pick inserted in center comes out clean.
- While cake is baking, prepare Orange Syrup (see below).

- Cool in pan on wire rack for 20 minutes.
- Remove cake from pan; invert cake, pecan crust-side-up onto a wire rack.
- While cake is cooling, bake Glazed Pecan Halves (see below).
- Brush top and sides of pound cake gently several times with hot Orange Syrup, using a pastry brush and allowing cake to absorb the Orange Syrup after each brushing. (Do not pour syrup over the cake).
- Let cake cool completely on wire rack.
- Arrange Glazed Pecan Halves around top of cake, if desired, or place on each piece as they are served.
- For Orange Syrup: Remove rind from orange with a vegetable peeler, being careful not to get the bitter white pith.
- Set orange rind aside.
- Squeeze orange to get 1/2 cup juice.
- Combine orange rind, juice and sugar in a small saucepan and cook over low heat, stirring until sugar dissolves.
- Bring mixture to a boil over medium high heat, and boil 2 minutes.
- Makes about 1 cup.
- For Glazed Pecan Halves: Combine pecan halves and corn syrup, stirring to coat pecans.
- Line a 15- x 10-inch jellyroll pan with parchment paper; coat with cooking spray.
- Arrange pecan halves in an even layer in a pan.
- Bake at 350°F for 12 minutes; stir using a rubber spatula.
- Remove from oven, stir, arrange in an even layer on wax paper and let cool completely.

Nutrition Information

- Calories: 1126.7
- Total Fat: 63.9
- Fiber: 5.3
- Cholesterol: 227.1
- Protein: 13.1
- Saturated Fat: 26.8
- Sodium: 365.3
- Sugar: 85.2

- Total Carbohydrate: 131.9

124.   Original Pound Cake

Serving: 1 cake | Prep: 10mins | Ready in:

Ingredients

- 2 cups sugar
- 2 cups flour
- 1/4 teaspoon salt
- 1 teaspoon baking soda
- 1 cup butter, softened
- 5 eggs
- 1 1/2 teaspoons vanilla extract
- 1 1/2 teaspoons lemon extract (optional)

Direction

- Combine all ingredients in a large mixer bowl until smooth about 5 or 6 minutes. Add eggs, one at a time while you mix.
- Pour into well buttered Bundt pan, or you can use a bread loaf pan.
- Bake at 325 for 60 minutes, or until cake tests done.

Nutrition Information

- Calories: 4471.2
- Sodium: 3503
- Sugar: 403.2
- Total Carbohydrate: 593.5
- Cholesterol: 1545.5
- Total Fat: 211.4
- Saturated Fat: 124.7
- Fiber: 6.8
- Protein: 59.2

125.　　Original Pound Cake From 1700's England

Serving: 20-24 serving(s) | Prep: 40mins | Ready in:

Ingredients

- 1 lb sugar (2 cups)
- 1 lb butter, room temp.
- 1 lb flour, sifted with salt ((4 cups before sifting)
- 1 dozen egg (12-10 depends how hen is laying today!)
- 1/4 teaspoon salt
- 1/4 cup fresh lemon juice
- 1 tablespoon fresh lemon rind, grated

Direction

- Preheat oven 325 degrees.
- In mixing bowl cream butter and sugar.
- Add 1 egg at a time, beating after each.
- Gradually add sifted flour, 1/2 cup at a time, til all blended.
- Add lemon juice and lemon rind, blend inches.
- Pour into a buttered and floured tube pan.
- Bake 1hr 15mins to 1hr 30 mins til toothpick in center comes out clean.

Nutrition Information

- Calories: 371.7
- Cholesterol: 147
- Protein: 5.9
- Saturated Fat: 12.5
- Fiber: 0.7
- Sugar: 22.9
- Total Carbohydrate: 40.5
- Total Fat: 21.1
- Sodium: 229.4

126.　　Papa's Apple Pound Cake

Serving: 6-8 serving(s) | Prep: 45mins | Ready in:

Ingredients

- 1/3 cup raisins
- 1 tablespoon dark rum
- 2 1/2 teaspoons dark rum
- 2 fuji apples, peeled and cored
- 1 cup all-purpose flour
- 3 tablespoons all-purpose flour (plus flour for the baking pan)
- 1/4 teaspoon baking powder
- 8 1/2 tablespoons unsalted butter, at room temperature (plus butter for the baking pan)
- 1 1/2 cups confectioners' sugar
- 3 large eggs, at room temperature
- 4 tablespoons apricot jam, melted and still warm

Direction

- Center a rack in the oven and pre-heat the oven to 350°F.
- Butter and flour an 8" x 4" x 2 and 1/2" loaf pan and fit a piece of parchment paper across the bottom of the pan, allowing an extra inch or two to drape over the opposite ends (this will allow for easy removal of the cake).
- Plump the raisins in a little boiling water, drain them well and place them to soak with a tablespoon of the rum.
- Cut one apple into 12 wedges and set aside.
- Cut the other apple into 8 wedges and then cut each of the 8 wedges in half crosswise and set aside.
- Sift together the flour and baking powder and set aside.
- In a mixing bowl, beat the butter until it is smooth.
- Slowly add one cup of the sugar and beat until creamy.
- Add the eggs one at a time, beating until mixture is well blended.
- Fold the sifter flour mixture into the egg mixture just until blended.
- Fold the raisins into the batter.
- Spoon half the batter into the prepared pan and smooth the top.

- Lay the 12 apple wedges down the center of the pan so that their sides touch and the domed side of each wedge is on top (there will be a thin strip of exposed batter on each side).
- Spoon the rest of the batter over and around the apples and again smooth the top.
- Arrange the halved apple slices in a single row along each long side of the pan, pressing the center cut sides of the apples against the sides of the pan.
- There will be two rows of apple slices, with their points towards the center of the pan, and exposed batter in the center.
- Gently push the apples into the batter, leaving the top of the apples exposed (mixture in the center of the pan will be slightly shallower than the sides).
- Let rest for ten minutes.
- Place pan in the oven and bake for ten minutes; using a sharp knife cut a slit down the center of the batter to help it rise evenly.
- Continue to bake until a knife inserted in the center comes out clean (another 40 to 50 minutes).
- Remove cake from oven and turn off oven.
- Gently brush the warm apricot jam over the hot cake and allow glaze to dry for five minutes.
- While the glaze is drying, combine the 2 and 1/2 teaspoons of rum and the 1/3 cup of confectioners' sugar in a small pan and warm over low heat, stirring until the icing is smooth.
- Brush the icing over the dried apricot glaze and return the cake, in its pan to the still warm oven just until the rum icing is dry--about two minutes.
- Place the cake, in its pan, on a rack until it cools to room temperature (keeping it in its pan will keep the cake moist).
- To remove the cake from the pan, lift it by the edges of the parchment paper, carefully remove the paper, and transfer to a platter.

Nutrition Information

- Calories: 483.9
- Saturated Fat: 11.2
- Fiber: 2.5
- Cholesterol: 136.2
- Total Fat: 19.1
- Sodium: 60.8
- Sugar: 46.4
- Total Carbohydrate: 72.3
- Protein: 6.3

127.   Passionfruit Pound Cake

Serving: 8-10 serving(s) | Prep: 10mins | Ready in:

Ingredients

- 1 lemon poundcake (Lemon Pound Cake)
- 1/2 cup passion fruit, unsweetened (puree or juice or nectar)
- 1/3 cup sugar
- powdered sugar
- whipping cream

Direction

- Make lemon pound cake the day before and refrigerate overnight.
- Put 1/2 cup passionfruit puree/juice/nectar in a nonreactive saucepan with the sugar.
- Bring to a boil just to dissolve the sugar.
- Cool.
- Sift powdered sugar (2-3 cups) into a bowl and slowly add sweetened passionfruit mixture a couple of tablespoons at a time until you have a thick glaze that is barely pourable.
- Pour out of bowl, drizzling all over the top of the pound cake.
- Take whipping cream and begin to whip at medium speed.
- Add sweetened passionfruit in sufficient quantity to flavor whipped cream.
- Serve slices of iced cake with flavored whipped cream.

Nutrition Information

- Calories: 192
- Sugar: 10
- Protein: 2.4
- Total Fat: 7.6
- Saturated Fat: 4.3
- Sodium: 153.4
- Fiber: 1.7
- Total Carbohydrate: 30.1
- Cholesterol: 82.9

128.   Paula Deen's Mama's Pound Cake

Serving: 15 serving(s) | Prep: 15mins | Ready in:

Ingredients

- 1 cup butter
- 1/2 cup Butter Flavor Crisco or 1/2 cup any shortening
- 3 cups sugar
- 5 eggs
- 3 cups all-purpose flour
- 1/2 teaspoon salt
- 1/2 teaspoon baking powder
- 1 cup milk
- 1 teaspoon vanilla extract

Direction

- Preheat oven to 350°.
- Grease flour a 10" tube pan or Bundt pan.
- Sift dry Ingredients.
- Cream butter shortening together.
- Add sugar a little at a time.
- Cream until fluffy.
- Add eggs one at a time, beating after each addition to fully incorporate the eggs into the batter.
- Add dry ingredients and milk to mixture alternating; starting and ending with flour.
- Mix in vanilla.
- Pour into prepared pan.

- Bake 1 to 1 1/2 hours, or until it passes the toothpick test.

Nutrition Information

- Calories: 450.9
- Sodium: 230.2
- Fiber: 0.7
- Cholesterol: 100.6
- Protein: 5.3
- Saturated Fat: 11.5
- Total Carbohydrate: 60
- Total Fat: 21.5
- Sugar: 40.1

129.   Peach Brandy Pound Cake

Serving: 1 Cake | Prep: 20mins | Ready in:

Ingredients

- CAKE
- 1 cup butter, at room temperature (no substitutes)
- 3 cups sugar
- 6 eggs
- 3 cups flour
- 1/4 teaspoon salt
- 1 cup sour cream
- 2 teaspoons rum
- 1 teaspoon orange extract
- 1/4 teaspoon almond extract
- 1/2 teaspoon lemon extract
- 1 teaspoon pure vanilla extract
- 1/2 cup peach brandy
- GLAZE (Optional)
- 1 1/4 cups powdered sugar
- 6 tablespoons peach brandy

Direction

- For Cake: Preheat oven to 325 degrees.

- Cream butter and sugar together, add eggs 1 at a time.
- Mix flour and salt and add alternately with sour cream.
- Stir in flavorings and brandy.
- Pour into a greased and floured Bundt pan.
- Bake 1 to 1-1/2 hours or until tests done.
- Cool cake in pan for 15 minutes, then remove to cool completely.
- Drizzle Glaze atop cake, if desired.
- For Glaze: Mix powdered sugar and brandy together and drizzle over cake.

Nutrition Information

- Calories: 6824.6
- Total Fat: 261.7
- Saturated Fat: 153
- Sodium: 2829.7
- Fiber: 10.1
- Sugar: 757
- Total Carbohydrate: 1045.9
- Cholesterol: 1723.7
- Protein: 83.1

130. Pecan Chocolate Chip Pound Cake

Serving: 16-20 serving(s) | Prep: 20mins | Ready in:

Ingredients

- 2 3/4 cups sugar
- 1 1/4 cups butter, softened (no substitutes)
- 5 eggs
- 1 teaspoon almond extract
- 3 cups all-purpose flour
- 1 teaspoon baking powder
- 1/4 teaspoon salt
- 1 cup milk
- 1 cup miniature semisweet chocolate chips
- 1 cup chopped pecans

Direction

- In a large mixing bowl, beat sugar, butter (must be very soft but not melted), eggs and almond extract on low just until mixed. Beat on high for 5 minutes, scraping bowl occasionally. In a separate bowl, combine flour, baking powder and salt. On low speed, add flour mixture alternately with milk, mixing just until blended. Fold in chocolate chips. Sprinkle pecans in the bottom of a greased and floured 10-in. tube pan. Carefully pour batter over pecans. Bake at 325° for 1 hour and 40 minutes or until cake tests done. Cool 20 minutes in pan before removing to a wire rack to cool completely.

Nutrition Information

- Calories: 478
- Fiber: 1.9
- Sugar: 40.7
- Total Carbohydrate: 61
- Protein: 6.1
- Total Fat: 24.9
- Saturated Fat: 12.3
- Sodium: 192.2
- Cholesterol: 106.4

131. Perfect Pound Cake

Serving: 16 serving(s) | Prep: 45mins | Ready in:

Ingredients

- 2 cups flour
- 1 cup sugar
- 1/2 cup butter
- 1/2 cup margarine
- 2 teaspoons baking powder
- 2/3 cup orange juice or 2/3 cup apricot juice
- 1 teaspoon vanilla
- 2 teaspoons rum (optional)
- 4 large eggs, separate

- 1/3 cup raisins or 1/3 cup almonds or 1/3 cup any dried fruit

Direction

- Preheat oven at 350°.
- At low speed cream butter, margarine, and sugar during 30 minutes (sound like a lot but trust me -- it's the key to the texture, meanwhile prepare the rest of the ingredients).
- Add the yolks to the mixture one by one, until they are incorporated in the mixture.
- In a separate bowl mix orange juice, vanilla and rum.
- Sift flour and baking soda, together.
- Alternating add to the mixture the flour and the juice.
- Add about a spoonful of flour to the raisins and cut them a bit, this will avoid to have raisins only at the bottom of the cake ;-).
- Set aside, and beat the egg whites until they are fluffy but not totally firm.
- With a wooden spoon mix the whites into the mixture.
- Pour into the mold (previously greased and floured) and spread it around leaving a small depression in the center, this way when it grows during baking it won't curve up.
- Bake for 35 minutes or until it is golden and the cake has separated from the mold.
- ENJOY!

Nutrition Information

- Calories: 239.9
- Sodium: 171
- Fiber: 0.6
- Sugar: 15.3
- Total Carbohydrate: 28.2
- Cholesterol: 68.1
- Protein: 3.5
- Total Fat: 12.9
- Saturated Fat: 5

132.   Philadelphia Cream Cheese Pound Cake

Serving: 12-14 serving(s) | Prep: 20mins | Ready in:

Ingredients

- 3/4 lb butter
- 1 (8 ounce) package Philadelphia Cream Cheese
- 3 cups sugar
- 6 eggs
- 3 cups cake flour
- 1 teaspoon vanilla flavoring

Direction

- Note: 3 sticks of butter equal 3/4 lb.
- All ingredients (including eggs and cream cheese) must be at room temperature.
- Cream butter well, add cream cheese.
- Mix thoroughly.
- Gradually add sugar.
- Add eggs, one at a time.
- Add flour gradually, then add vanilla flavor.
- Place cake in tube pan in COLD oven.
- Bake at 325 degrees F (163 degrees C) for 1 1/2 hours (gas oven 1 hour) [from the time you turn on the oven].
- Note: The longer the cream cheese, butter, and eggs sit at room temperature, the better the cake (ingredients can be left out overnight).

Nutrition Information

- Calories: 622.3
- Sugar: 50.7
- Cholesterol: 174.8
- Sodium: 300.1
- Fiber: 0.6
- Total Carbohydrate: 77.7
- Protein: 7.3
- Total Fat: 32.2
- Saturated Fat: 19.1

133. Pineapple Orange Pound Cake

Serving: 12-16 serving(s) | Prep: 10mins | Ready in:

Ingredients

- CAKE
- 19 1/4 ounces supreme pineapple cake mix
- 3 ounces vanilla instant pudding mix
- 4 large eggs
- 1 cup orange juice
- 1/3 cup vegetable oil
- 1 tablespoon orange zest
- GLAZE
- 1/3 cup granulated sugar
- 1/4 cup orange juice

Direction

- Preheat oven to 350*.Grease and flour 10" Bundt pan -- set aside.
- FOR CAKE:
- Combine cake mix, pudding mix, eggs, 1 cup orange juice, oil and orange peel in large bowl.
- Beat at medium speed with electric mixer for 2 minutes.
- Pour into pan.
- Bake at 350* for 50-60 minutes or until toothpick inserted near the center comes out clean.
- Cool 25 minutes in pan.
- Invert onto serving plate.
- FOR GLAZE:
- Combine sugar and 1/4 cup orange juice in small pan --
- Simmer 3 minutes.
- Brush warm glaze over cake.

Nutrition Information

- Calories: 138.2
- Sodium: 125.6
- Total Carbohydrate: 15.1
- Cholesterol: 70.5
- Protein: 2.3
- Total Fat: 7.8
- Fiber: 0.1
- Sugar: 14.4
- Saturated Fat: 1.3

134. Pound Cake Pound Cake

Serving: 12 serving(s) | Prep: 0S | Ready in:

Ingredients

- 1 cup butter
- 1 cup margarine
- 3 cups sugar
- 5 eggs
- 1 teaspoon lemon flavoring
- 1 cup sweet milk
- 3 cups plain flour
- 1 teaspoon vanilla

Direction

- Cream butter, margarine and sugar. Add eggs, one at a time. Add vanilla and lemon flavoring. Add milk and flour.
- Bake at 350F for 45 minutes to an hour or until done.

Nutrition Information

- Calories: 621.9
- Total Fat: 33.5
- Fiber: 0.8
- Sugar: 51.3
- Protein: 6.8
- Saturated Fat: 13.4
- Sodium: 324.2
- Total Carbohydrate: 75.1
- Cholesterol: 130.8

135. Pound Cake With Brown Sugar Frosting

Serving: 1 cake, 14 serving(s) | Prep: 0S | Ready in:

Ingredients

- CAKE
- 6 cups sifted cake flour (not self-rising, plus more for pans)
- 1 1/2 teaspoons salt
- 2 1/4 tablespoons baking powder
- 1 lb unsalted butter, plus 4 tablespoons unsalted butter (plus more for pans, room temperature)
- 2 1/2 cups lightly packed light-brown sugar
- 12 large eggs, divided
- 1 1/2 cups milk
- 1 tablespoon pure vanilla extract
- FROSTING
- 1 1/4 cups lightly packed light-brown sugar
- 5 large egg whites
- 2 cups unsalted butter, room temperature
- 1 teaspoon pure vanilla extract

Direction

- CAKE:
- Preheat oven to 325 degrees Fahrenheit.
- Butter and flour two 8-by-3-inch square cake pans.
- Line pans with parchment paper; set aside.
- In a bowl, sift together flour, salt, and baking powder; set aside.
- In the bowl of an electric mixer fitted with the paddle attachment, combine unsalted butter and light-brown sugar.
- Beat on medium high until fluffy, about 10 minutes.
- Add eggs, one at a time, beating well after each addition
- Add flour mixture to egg mixture, alternating with milk, in three additions, beginning and ending with the flour.
- Stir in vanilla extract.
- Pour batter into prepared pans.

- Smooth the tops; bake until a cake tester inserted in center comes out clean, about 90 minutes.
- Rotate pans after 45 minutes to promote even baking.
- Transfer to a cooling rack.
- Cool in pans 10 minutes.
- Remove from pans; cool completely while making brown-sugar-meringue buttercream frosting.
- ASSEMBLE CAKE:
- Using a serrated knife, trim cakes so each is level, even, and about 2 inches high.
- Cut one cake into a 6-inch square; set aside.
- Reserve excess cake for another use.
- Cut second cake into two smaller squares, one 3-3/4 inches and the other 2-1/4 inches.
- Brush top and sides of each cake with a pastry brush to remove crumbs; set aside.
- From a sturdy piece of cardboard, or 3/16-inch foam board, cut out one cake board for each layer.
- Place trimmed layers onto their corresponding boards.
- Using an offset spatula, coat each cake with a thin layer of buttercream to seal in the crumbs.
- Chill in the refrigerator until firm, about 20 minutes.
- Transfer 3/4 cup buttercream to a pastry bag fitted with a number 5 plain round tip; set aside.
- With remaining buttercream, cover each layer with a final coat of buttercream, using an offset spatula to smooth the icing.
- Place cakes in refrigerator to set, about 20 minutes.
- Loosen the middle-size cake from its base; carefully center it on the larger cake.
- Repeat with smallest cake.
- Pipe dot design on cake; chill if not serving immediately.
- Remove from refrigerator at least 30 minutes and up to 3 hours before serving.
- FOR THE FROSTING:
- In the heat-proof bowl of an electric mixer, combine light-brown sugar and egg whites.

- Place the bowl over a pot of gently simmering water; whisk until mixture becomes hot to the touch, about 5 minutes.
- Return bowl to mixer stand. Whip mixture with the whisk attachment until cooled, about 12 minutes.
- Switch to paddle attachment; add butter 1 tablespoon at a time.
- Stir in vanilla.
- If not using immediately, transfer to an airtight container, and store at room temperature up to 8 hours.

Nutrition Information

- Calories: 990.3
- Sodium: 548
- Cholesterol: 324.4
- Total Carbohydrate: 105.5
- Protein: 12.9
- Total Fat: 58.4
- Saturated Fat: 35.3
- Fiber: 1
- Sugar: 57.5

136.   Pound Cake With Caramel Icing Apricot Ginger Sprinkles

Serving: 16 serving(s) | Prep: 20mins | Ready in:

Ingredients

- POUND CAKE
- 1 1/2 cups butter or 1 1/2 cups margarine, softened
- 2 1/2 cups granulated sugar
- 1/2 cup firmly packed light brown sugar
- 6 large eggs
- 3 cups all-purpose flour
- 1/2 teaspoon salt
- 1/4 teaspoon baking soda
- 8 ounces container sour cream
- 2 teaspoons vanilla extract
- CARAMEL ICING
- 1 1/4 cups firmly packed light brown sugar
- 5 tablespoons heavy cream
- 1/4 cup butter
- 1 dash salt
- 1/2 teaspoon vanilla extract
- APRICOT-GINGER SPRINKLES
- 1/2 cup salted cashews
- 1/3 cup finely chopped dried apricot
- 3 tablespoons minced crystallized ginger

Direction

- POUND CAKE:
- Beat butter at medium speed with an electric mixer until creamy.
- Gradually add sugars, beating at medium speed until light and fluffy.
- Add eggs, 1 at a time, beating just until yellow disappears after each addition.
- Stir together flour, salt, and baking soda.
- Add to butter mixture alternately with sour cream, beginning and ending with flour mixture.
- Beat at low speed just until blended after each addition.
- Stir in vanilla.
- Pour into 2 greased and floured 9- x 5-inch loaf pans.
- Bake at 325°F for 1 hour to 1 hour and 10 minutes or until a wooden pick inserted in center comes out clean.
- Cool in pans on a wire rack 10 minutes.
- Remove cakes from pans, and let cool 2 hours or until completely cool.
- PREPARE CARAMEL ICING:
- Bring first 4 ingredients to a full rolling boil in a medium saucepan over medium heat, stirring often.
- Boil, stirring constantly, 1 minute.
- Remove from heat; stir in vanilla.
- Beat at medium speed with an electric mixer 2 to 4 minutes or until thickened.
- Use immediately.
- Pour over cake, allowing it to drip down sides of cake.

- APRICOT-GINGER SPRINKLES:
- Toss all ingredients together, and top pound cake no more than one hour before serving.
- Let stand 30 minutes or until icing is firm.
- Enjoy!

Nutrition Information

- Calories: 580.5
- Protein: 6.2
- Fiber: 1
- Saturated Fat: 16.6
- Sodium: 354.9
- Sugar: 57
- Total Carbohydrate: 76.6
- Cholesterol: 137.3
- Total Fat: 28.8

---

137. Pound Cake With Granola

Serving: 12 serving(s) | Prep: 10mins | Ready in:

Ingredients

- 1 yellow cake mix
- 1/4 cup water
- 1/4 cup oil
- 8 ounces plain yogurt
- 3 eggs
- 1 cup granola cereal
- GLAZE
- 1/2 cup powdered sugar
- 2 1/2 teaspoons water

Direction

- Heat oven to 350F degrees.
- Grease and flour 10inch tube pan.
- In large bowl, combine cake mix, water, oil, yogurt, and eggs.
- Beat 2 minutes at high speed.
- Pour half the batter in pan.
- Sprinkle with 1/2 cup granola.

- Spread remaining batter over granola, and sprinkle with remaining granola.
- Bake for 50-55 minutes Use the toothpick test.
- Cool in pan 30 minutes, then invert onto cake plate.
- For glaze, mix powdered sugar and water until smooth.
- Drizzle over warm cake.

Nutrition Information

- Calories: 328.9
- Saturated Fat: 2.6
- Sodium: 316.2
- Sugar: 26.9
- Total Fat: 14
- Fiber: 1.4
- Total Carbohydrate: 45.5
- Cholesterol: 56.4
- Protein: 5.7

---

138. Pound Cake With Ruby Cranberry Sauce

Serving: 1 pound cake, 4-6 serving(s) | Prep: 5mins | Ready in:

Ingredients

- 1 store bought poundcake (We used Sara Lee)
- 3 cups fresh cranberries or 3 cups thawed frozen cranberries
- 1 cup sugar
- 1/2 cup water
- 1 -2 tablespoon brandy or 2 teaspoons brandy extract
- brandy sweetened whipping cream, garnish
- toasted slivered almonds, garnish
- 1 sprig mint, garnish

Direction

- Stir cranberries, sugar and water in 2-qt saucepan.

- Cook over medium heat until mixture comes to a boil, about 5-10 minutes.
- Continue cooking, stirring occasionally, until cranberries pop, about 3-4 minutes.
- Cool 30 minutes.
- Stir in brandy.
- Place in microwave-safe bowl.
- Cover; refrigerate until serving time.
- Just before serving, microwave sauce on HIGH, stirring once, until warm (1-2 mins).
- Use 2 tablespoons sauce over each serving or slice of cake.
- Garnish with sweetened whipped cream or frozen topping, almond slivers, and sprig of mint.

Nutrition Information

- Calories: 527.5
- Saturated Fat: 8.7
- Sugar: 52.8
- Total Fat: 15
- Sodium: 300.6
- Fiber: 3.6
- Total Carbohydrate: 95.3
- Cholesterol: 165.8
- Protein: 4.4

139.   Pound Cake With Tropical Fruit And Rum Apricot Sauce

Serving: 6 serving(s) | Prep: 5mins | Ready in:

Ingredients

- 1 cup apricot jam
- 1/2 cup water
- 1 tablespoon rum
- 2 mangoes, peeled, halved and thinly sliced
- 4 kiwi fruits, peeled and sliced
- 1 lb cake, sliced
- 1 cup whipped cream

Direction

- In a medium saucepan, mix the apricot jam with the water, rum and fruit. Bring to a boil over medium heat. Boil until sauce is thickened and syrupy, about 5 minutes. Cool slightly.
- To serve: place a slice or two of pound cake in serving plate, top with some fruit and syrup. Garnish with a dollop of whipped cream.

Nutrition Information

- Calories: 235.8
- Sodium: 37.6
- Cholesterol: 7.6
- Protein: 1.6
- Total Fat: 2.8
- Saturated Fat: 1.4
- Fiber: 2.9
- Sugar: 35.2
- Total Carbohydrate: 54.8

140.   Pumpkin Chocolate Chip Pound Cake

Serving: 8 serving(s) | Prep: 45mins | Ready in:

Ingredients

- 1 3/4 cups unbleached all-purpose flour
- 1 teaspoon baking soda
- 1 teaspoon baking powder
- 1 teaspoon ground cinnamon
- 1/2 teaspoon salt
- 1/4 teaspoon ground cloves
- nutmeg, a pinch
- 1/2 cup unsalted butter, softened
- 1 1/4 cups sugar
- 3 large eggs
- 1 cup canned pumpkin
- 1 teaspoon pure vanilla extract
- 1/3 cup milk
- 1 cup miniature semisweet chocolate chips

- 1 cup chopped walnuts

Direction

- Preheat oven to 350°; coat the inside of a 9x5 inch loaf pan with nonstick cooking spray and dust it with flour.
- In a bowl, combine the flour, baking soda, baking powder, cinnamon, salt, cloves, and nutmeg; set aside.
- In a large mixing bowl, combine the butter and sugar; cream with an electric mixer on med-high speed until fluffy, about 3 minutes, scrape down the sides of bowl as needed.
- With the mixer on med-low speed, add the eggs, one at a time, scraping down the sides of bowl after each addition; stir in the pumpkin and vanilla; stir in the milk.
- Turn the mixer to low speed and add the flour mixture 1/2 cup at a time, scraping down the sides of the bowl after each addition.
- Stir in the chocolate chips and walnuts.
- Scrape batter into prepared pan and smooth the top with a rubber spatula.
- Bake for 55 minutes - 1hour, until the cake is firm to the touch and a pick comes out clean.
- Let the cake cool in the pan for 5 minutes, invert it onto a wire rack, and then turn it right side up on a rack to cool completely.
- Store uneaten cake in a cake keeper at room temperature for up to 3 days or in the refrigerator, wrapped in plastic, for up to 1 week.

Nutrition Information

- Calories: 568.7
- Total Fat: 30.1
- Fiber: 4.1
- Total Carbohydrate: 71.3
- Protein: 9.1
- Saturated Fat: 12.9
- Sodium: 458.1
- Sugar: 44.7
- Cholesterol: 111.2

141.   Quatre Quarts Aux Pommes: (Apple Upside Down Pound Cake)

Serving: 6 serving(s) | Prep: 15mins | Ready in:

Ingredients

- 3 nice tart apples
- 15 sugar cubes
- 2 large eggs
- 1/2 cup granulated sugar
- 1/2 cup flour
- 1/2 cup butter, softened
- 1 teaspoon baking powder

Direction

- Preheat oven to 410°F (210°C).
- In a non-stick saucepan, make a caramel sauce using the sugar cubes and 2 or 3 spoonfuls of water.
- Once the caramel has reached a golden brown or "blond" color, pour in into a cake pan.
- Tilt and rotate the pan so that the bottom is evenly covered with the caramel.
- Peel the apples and cut them into large wedges.
- Place the wedges onto the caramel.
- Mix butter and sugar in a large bowl.
- Add the eggs one at a time, then the flour and baking powder.
- Mix well.
- Pour batter over the apples.
- Bake 30-40 minutes.
- Let cool before removing from pan.

Nutrition Information

- Calories: 321.1
- Sodium: 193.7
- Sugar: 29.7
- Cholesterol: 111.2
- Protein: 3.5
- Total Fat: 17.2

- Saturated Fat: 10.3
- Fiber: 1.9
- Total Carbohydrate: 40.2

142.   Rae Simpson's World Famous Pound Cake

Serving: 1 cake | Prep: 20mins | Ready in:

Ingredients

- 1 cup heavy whipping cream
- 1/2 teaspoon salt
- 3 cups sifted cake flour
- 1 cup unsalted butter, at room temperature
- 1 tablespoon pure vanilla extract
- 3 cups granulated sugar
- 6 large eggs, at room temperature

Direction

- Set an oven rack in the middle position and reposition the remaining rack below it.
- Preheat the oven to 325 degrees.
- Generously butter a 9-inch removable-bottom tube pan.
- Heat cream and salt on low heat only enough to dissolve salt. Flour needs to be sifted BEFORE measuring.
- Whip the butter on high speed until creamy; add the vanilla and whip until well-blended.
- Gradually add the sugar, then whip the butter and sugar on high speed for several minutes, or until the mixture is airy and turns whitish.
- Reduce the speed to slow and add the eggs, one at a time, mixing thoroughly between additions.
- Stop the mixer and scrape down the sides after every other egg.
- Now stop mixing.
- Remove the mixing bowl from the stand (if you are using one) and sift about one-quarter of the flour into the mixture through a strainer or sifter.

- Replace the bowl and thoroughly mix the flour into the batter on low speed.
- Drizzle in about one third of cream, mixing until thoroughly incorporated.
- Continue to alternate, sifting in flour and drizzling in cream, ending with the flour.
- When the last of the flour has been added, scrape down the mixture and beat for a few more seconds just to make sure that everything is well-incorporated.
- Remove the bowl from the stand and scrape the batter into the prepared tube pan.
- Run a knife through the batter to break up any air pockets, and then smooth the top of the batter.
- Bake the cake on the middle rack for 1 1/2 hours, turning it from front to back after about one hour for even browning.
- The cake should be well-browned, with a golden, crackling top, when fully baked.
- Stick a toothpick in the cake, if desired, to test it; the toothpick should come out clean if the cake is fully baked.
- Let the cake cool on a rack for 20 minutes, then remove the cake from the pan, running a knife around the edges if it sticks, and let it cool upside down on a cooling rack.
- Refrigerate overnight before serving.

Nutrition Information

- Calories: 6724.9
- Total Fat: 304.2
- Sodium: 1719.5
- Total Carbohydrate: 931.2
- Protein: 78.2
- Saturated Fat: 181.3
- Fiber: 7
- Sugar: 603.2
- Cholesterol: 1930.1

143.   Red Velvet Pecan Praline Pound Cake

Serving: 8-10 serving(s) | Prep: 30mins | Ready in:

Ingredients

- Pecan Praline Powder
- 1/2 cup warm water
- 1/2 cup granulated sugar
- 1/2 cup pecans, toasted and chopped
- Red Velvet Pound Cake
- 1/3 cup untoasted pecans, finely chopped
- 1/2 cup butter, softened
- 1/2 cup vegetable shortening
- 2 cups granulated sugar
- 6 large eggs
- 1 ounce red food coloring
- 2 teaspoons vanilla extract
- 2 1/2 cups all-purpose flour
- 1/2 cup dark cocoa
- 1/2 teaspoon baking powder
- 1 cup buttermilk
- 1/2 cup miniature chocolate chip

Direction

- To make Pecan Praline Powder:
- Prepare a jelly roll pan by lining with foil and buttering the bottom.
- Combine 1/2 cup water with 1/2 cup granulated sugar in a heavy bottomed skillet over high heat and cook until the mixture begins to turn a light caramel color (about 8 minutes). When sugar becomes caramel colored, quickly add 1/2 cup toasted chopped pecans and mix with a wooden spoon until nuts are covered with caramel.
- Take off heat and immediately pour mixture onto the buttered foil-lined jelly roll pan, spreading out the hot sugar-nut mixture. Allow it to cool. Once it cools completely, break it into pieces and pulverize in a food processor. Grind it a bit coarsely, so you can see nut bits, but that is a personal preference. Set aside. Makes about 2/3 cup.

- To Make Pound Cake: Preheat oven to 300 degree F.
- Grease, flour and sprinkle with finely chopped pecans (1/3 cup untoasted) a 10-inch tube pan.
- Cream together butter, shortening and sugar until fluffy. Blend in eggs one at a time, beating well after each addition.
- Add red food coloring and vanilla extract. In another bowl stir together flour, cocoa powder and baking powder.
- Beat flour mixture in three parts into creamed mixture, alternating with buttermilk. Begin and end with flour. Stir in chocolate chips and Pecan Praline Powder.
- Pour batter into prepared pan. Bake for 1 hour and 15 minutes or until toothpick tests clean. Cool 15 minutes in pan, then invert onto serving plate and allow to cool completely before serving. Dust with cocoa powder or confectioners' sugar for a pretty presentation.

Nutrition Information

- Calories: 818.4
- Saturated Fat: 15
- Sodium: 212.5
- Sugar: 70.6
- Total Carbohydrate: 105.7
- Cholesterol: 171.2
- Total Fat: 40.5
- Fiber: 3.8
- Protein: 12.4

144.   Red Velvet Pound Cake

Serving: 8-12 serving(s) | Prep: 20mins | Ready in:

Ingredients

- Cake
- 3 cups unsifted flour
- 3/4 cup milk
- 3 cups sugar
- 1 ounce red food coloring

- 3/4 cup shortening
- 7 eggs
- 1/2 cup butter
- 1 teaspoon baking powder
- 1 tablespoon vanilla
- 1/4 teaspoon salt
- 1/2 cup cocoa
- Icing
- 8 ounces cream cheese, soft
- 1/2 cup confectioners' sugar, plus
- 2 tablespoons confectioners' sugar
- 1 teaspoon vanilla
- 1/2 butter, soft

Direction

- CAKE: Cream sugar, shortening, vanilla, food coloring and eggs.
- Add dry ingredients and milk.
- Bake in large and floured tube pan for 1-1/2 hours at 275 degrees.
- Turn out of pan to cool.
- ICING: Cream together cream cheese, sugar, vanilla and butter.
- Spread over cooled cake.

Nutrition Information

- Calories: 965.9
- Sugar: 85.1
- Total Carbohydrate: 125.7
- Cholesterol: 249.9
- Total Fat: 47
- Saturated Fat: 20.7
- Fiber: 3
- Sodium: 358.5
- Protein: 14.4

145.   Rich Chocolate Pound Cake

Serving: 16 serving(s) | Prep: 15mins | Ready in:

Ingredients

- 2 cups semi-sweet chocolate chips, divided
- 3 cups all-purpose flour
- 1 tablespoon baking powder
- 1/2 teaspoon salt
- 2 cups light brown sugar, packed
- 1 cup margarine, softened
- 1 tablespoon vanilla extract
- 4 large eggs, room temperature
- 1/2 cup milk

Direction

- Preheat oven to 350° F.
- Grease 10-inch Bundt pan.
- Microwave 1 1/2 cups morsels in medium, uncovered, microwave-safe bowl on HIGH (100%) power for 1 minute; STIR.
- (The morsels may retain some of their original shape.).
- If necessary, microwave at additional 10- to 15-second intervals, stirring just until morsels are melted.
- Cool to room temperature.
- Combine flour, baking powder and salt in medium bowl.
- Beat sugar, butter and vanilla extract in large mixer bowl until creamy.
- Add eggs one at a time, beating well after each addition.
- Beat in melted chocolate.
- Gradually beat in flour mixture alternately with milk.
- Spoon into prepared Bundt pan.
- Bake for 55 to 65 minutes or until wooden pick inserted in cake comes out clean.
- Cool in pan for 30 minutes.
- Invert cake onto wire rack to cool completely.
- MICROWAVE remaining morsels in heavy-duty plastic bag on HIGH (100%) power for 45 seconds; knead bag.
- Microwave at additional 10- to 15-second intervals, kneading until smooth.
- Cut a small hole in corner of bag; squeeze to drizzle over cake.

Nutrition Information

- Calories: 417
- Fiber: 1.9
- Sugar: 38.2
- Total Fat: 19.4
- Saturated Fat: 6.3
- Sodium: 308.5
- Total Carbohydrate: 58.8
- Cholesterol: 53.9
- Protein: 5.2

146.   Rich Decadent Pound Cake

Serving: 12 , 12 serving(s) | Prep: 2hours | Ready in:

Ingredients

- 1 cup butter, room temperature
- 1 2/3 cups granulated sugar
- 5 eggs, room temperature
- 2 cups flour
- 1 teaspoon vanilla
- 1 dash salt (1/8 t.)

Direction

- Preheat oven to 300 degrees. Grease one large, or two small, loaf pans and set aside.
- Make sure butter and eggs are at room temperature, with butter very soft (but not melted).
- Cream butter in mixer until well whipped. Slowly add sugar and combine thoroughly.
- Add eggs one at a time, beating for 2 full minutes after each egg is added.
- Slowly add flour and mix just until blended. Add vanilla and salt.
- Pour mixture into loaf pan(s). Bake 1 hour and 30 minutes if using large loaf pan, or 1 hour if using 2 small loaf pans. Cake is done when toothpick inserted in center comes out clean.
- Put pans on rack and cool for 10 minutes. Run knife along edge of loaf pan, tap bottom of the

pan on the counter, and "unmold" cake. Put cake on rack to cool completely.

Nutrition Information

- Calories: 349.8
- Fiber: 0.6
- Total Carbohydrate: 43.9
- Protein: 4.9
- Total Fat: 17.5
- Saturated Fat: 10.4
- Sodium: 178.3
- Sugar: 27.9
- Cholesterol: 118.2

147.   Ricotta Orange Pound Cake

Serving: 8 slices, 8 serving(s) | Prep: 15mins | Ready in:

Ingredients

- 1 1/2 cups cake flour
- 2 1/2 teaspoons baking powder
- 1 teaspoon kosher salt
- 3/4 cup butter, room temperature, plus more to grease the baking pan
- 1 1/2 cups whole milk ricotta cheese
- 1 1/2 cups sugar, plus 1 tablespoon
- 3 large eggs
- 1 teaspoon vanilla extract
- 1 orange, zested
- 2 tablespoons Amaretto
- 2 tablespoons powdered sugar, for dusting
- 2 cups strawberries, hulled and quartered

Direction

- Preheat the oven to 350 degrees F. Grease a 9 by 5 by 3-inch loaf pan with butter. In a medium bowl combine the flour, baking powder, and salt. Stir to combine.
- Using an electric mixer, cream together the butter, ricotta, and sugar until light and fluffy,

about 3 minutes. With the machine running, add the eggs 1 at a time. Add the vanilla, orange zest, and Amaretto until combined. Add the dry ingredients, a small amount at a time, until just incorporated. Pour the mixture into the prepared pan and bake until a toothpick comes out clean and the cake is beginning to pull away from the sides of the pan, about 45 to 50 minutes. Let the cake cool in the pan for 10 minutes then transfer to a wire rack to cool completely. Using a mesh sieve, dust the cooled cake with powdered sugar.

- Meanwhile, place the strawberries (or orange supremes) in a small bowl with the remaining 1 tablespoon sugar. Let sit until the juices have pooled around the strawberries.
- To serve, slice the cake and serve with a spoonful of strawberries and their juices over the top of the cake.

Nutrition Information

- Calories: 527.8
- Sodium: 520
- Fiber: 1.6
- Sugar: 43.1
- Total Carbohydrate: 66.2
- Cholesterol: 148.6
- Total Fat: 25.5
- Saturated Fat: 15.4
- Protein: 10.2

148. SOUL FOOD SWEET POTATO POUND CAKE

Serving: 8 serving(s) | Prep: 15mins | Ready in:

Ingredients

- 1/2 cup walnuts, chopped
- 3 cups cake flour, sifted
- 2 cups Splenda sugar substitute, Sugar Substitute (granular)

- 1 teaspoon baking powder
- 1/2 teaspoon salt
- 1/4 teaspoon baking soda
- 1 cup butter, softened
- 1 cup sweet potato, cooked and mashed
- 1 cup low-fat buttermilk
- 1 teaspoon lemon extract
- 1 teaspoon vanilla extract
- 6 large eggs

Direction

- Preheat oven to 350° F.
- Grease and flour a 10-inch Bundt pan. Sprinkle walnuts in pan; set aside.
- Combine flour, sugar or sugar substitute, baking powder, salt and soda in a large bowl; set aside.
- Beat butter at medium speed with an electric mixer for about two minutes or until creamy.
- Add sweet potatoes, buttermilk and extracts, beating until blended.
- Add flour mixture in thirds, beating until batter is smooth after each addition.
- Add eggs, one at a time, beating just until yellow disappears.
- Spoon batter into prepared pan.
- Bake 50 to 60 minutes or until a long wooden pick inserted in the center comes out clean.
- Cool in pan on a wire rack 10 to 15 minutes; remove from pan, and cool on a wire rack.
- Remove from pan nut side up.

Nutrition Information

- Calories: 568.9
- Saturated Fat: 16.4
- Sodium: 528.5
- Fiber: 1.9
- Sugar: 14.3
- Cholesterol: 201.7
- Total Fat: 32.1
- Total Carbohydrate: 59.5
- Protein: 11.6

149. Sam's Toasted Pound Cake With Raspberries

Serving: 4 serving(s) | Prep: 5mins | Ready in:

Ingredients

- 4 slices poundcake, 1-inch thick
- 1 pint raspberries
- 1/2 pint whipping cream
- 2 tablespoons Chambord raspberry liquor

Direction

- Add Chambord raspberry liqueur to whipping cream and whip.
- Toast pound cake slices.
- Place a slice of toasted pound cake on plate, add some whipped cream and top with some berries.

Nutrition Information

- Calories: 362.2
- Sodium: 142.8
- Cholesterol: 147.8
- Total Carbohydrate: 25.6
- Protein: 3.8
- Total Fat: 28.5
- Saturated Fat: 17.2
- Fiber: 5.2
- Sugar: 3.5

150. Seven Flavor Pound Cake

Serving: 1 cake | Prep: 10mins | Ready in:

Ingredients

- CAKE
- 18 1/2 ounces Duncan Hines yellow cake mix
- 3 eggs
- 1/3 cup vegetable oil
- 1 1/3 cups milk
- 1 teaspoon lemon extract
- 1 teaspoon rum extract
- 1 teaspoon vanilla extract
- 1 teaspoon orange extract
- 1 teaspoon coconut extract
- 1 teaspoon pineapple extract
- 1 teaspoon butter flavor extract
- GLAZE
- 1 cup sugar
- 1/2 cup water
- 1 teaspoon lemon extract
- 1 teaspoon rum extract
- 1 teaspoon vanilla extract
- 1 teaspoon orange extract
- 1 teaspoon coconut extract
- 1 teaspoon pineapple extract
- 1 teaspoon butter flavor extract

Direction

- Preheat oven to 350 degrees.
- Grease and flour a Bundt pan (I use Baker's Joy Spray).
- Measure all extracts into measuring cup, then add milk to equal 1 1/3 cup of liquid, and then make cake as directed on box.
- Pour batter into prepared Bundt pan.
- Bake for 38-43 minutes or until cake separates from side of pan.
- Cool cake.
- Prepare glaze: Combine all glaze ingredients in small pan and cook over low heat until sugar dissolves.
- Pour glaze over cake.

Nutrition Information

- Calories: 4288.6
- Saturated Fat: 30.6
- Fiber: 5.8
- Sugar: 435.3
- Cholesterol: 690.6
- Protein: 52.8
- Total Fat: 160.8
- Sodium: 3848.9

- Total Carbohydrate: 634.8

---

151. Smoothest Southern Pound Cake

Serving: 1 10-inch cake | Prep: 0S | Ready in:

Ingredients

- 1 cup butter or 1 cup margarine, softened
- 3 cups sugar
- 3 cups sifted cake flour
- 1/4 teaspoon baking soda
- 6 large eggs
- 1 (8 ounce) carton sour cream
- 1 teaspoon vanilla extract

Direction

- Beat butter at medium speed with an electric mixer (not a hand held one) about 2 minutes or until creamy. Gradually add sugar, beating at medium speed 5 to 7 minutes. Combine cake flour and baking soda, and add to butter mixture 1 cup at a time. (Batter will be extremely thick).
- Separate eggs; add yolks to batter, and mix well. Stir in sour cream and vanilla. Beat egg whites until stiff, and fold into batter.
- Spoon into a greased and floured 12-cup Bundt or 10-inch tube pan. Bake at 300F for 2 hours or until a wooden pick inserted in the center comes out clean. (You may also spoon batter into two 9- x 5- x 3-inch loaf pans; bake at 300F for 1 1/2 hours or until a wooden pick inserted in center comes out clean). Cool in pan on wire rack 10 to 15 minutes. Remove from pan; cool completely on wire rack.
- NOTE: Standard Mixing Method: If you are using a handheld mixer or prefer a conventional pound cake method, here's the procedure we suggest.
- Beat butter at medium speed with an electric mixer about 2 minutes or until creamy. Gradually add 3 cups sugar, beating at

medium speed 5 to 7 minutes. Add eggs, one at a time, beating just until yellow disappears.
- Combine cake flour and baking soda; add to butter mixture alternately with sour cream, beginning and ending with flour mixture. Mix at lowest speed just until mixture is blended after each addition. Stir in vanilla. Bake as directed.

Nutrition Information

- Calories: 6340.2
- Total Fat: 263.4
- Saturated Fat: 154
- Fiber: 7
- Sodium: 2567.4
- Sugar: 610.2
- Total Carbohydrate: 930.3
- Cholesterol: 1728.4
- Protein: 78.3

---

152. Soul Warming Pound Cake

Serving: 2 cakes, 6-8 serving(s) | Prep: 15mins | Ready in:

Ingredients

- 5 large eggs, beaten
- 1 cup butter, melted
- 2 cups flour
- 2 cups sugar
- 1/2 cup milk
- 1 tablespoon vanilla flavoring

Direction

- Beat butter in sugar in large bowl until smooth and creamy with hand mixer.
- Add eggs, a small amount at a time, and beat well after each addition.

- When all of eggs are mixed in, add vanilla flavoring, milk and flour and beat until all ingredients are combined.
- Grease and flour 2 loaf pans. Pour batter into each pan until it is about ¾ full.
- Place in 350 degrees Fahrenheit oven. Bake until toothpick inserted into cake comes out clean (approximately 15-25 minutes).
- Let cake cool for 5 minutes, then carefully invert onto large plate or platter.
- Slice cake into desired thickness and serve warm.

Nutrition Information

- Calories: 760.3
- Protein: 10.5
- Total Fat: 36
- Saturated Fat: 21.2
- Sodium: 287.1
- Cholesterol: 260.4
- Fiber: 1.1
- Sugar: 67.1
- Total Carbohydrate: 99.8

153. Southern Pound Cake

Serving: 1 cake | Prep: 15mins | Ready in:

Ingredients

- 2 cups cake flour
- 2 cups sugar
- 1 cup Crisco
- 5 large eggs
- 1/4 cup milk
- 1 tablespoon vanilla

Direction

- Preheat oven to 350.
- Grease and flour a tube pan.
- Cream sugar and Crisco well. Add eggs, 1 at a time, beating after each egg.

- Alternately add flour, milk and vanilla, beating after each addition.
- Pour into greased and floured tube pan.
- Bake for 1 hour and 10 minutes. Cool 10 minutes in pan, then invert onto cooling rack.

Nutrition Information

- Calories: 4796.1
- Total Fat: 234.4
- Saturated Fat: 71.8
- Sodium: 386.5
- Fiber: 4.7
- Sugar: 404.1
- Total Carbohydrate: 620.1
- Cholesterol: 1066
- Protein: 55.9

154. State Fair Pound Cake

Serving: 12 serving(s) | Prep: 15mins | Ready in:

Ingredients

- 1 cup butter
- 1/2 cup shortening
- 3 cups sugar
- 6 eggs
- 1 teaspoon coconut flavoring
- 1 teaspoon butternut flavoring
- 3 cups cake flour
- 1/2 teaspoon baking powder
- 1 cup milk

Direction

- Preheat oven to 325°F
- Have all ingredients at room temperature.
- In a mixing bowl, cream butter, shortening and sugar until light and fluffy.
- Add eggs, one at a time, and beat well.
- Add coconut and butternut flavoring.
- Sift together flour and baking powder in a bowl.

- Alternately add flour mixture and milk into creamed mixture; mix until combined.
- Pour batter into a greased and floured tube pan.
- Bake 1 3/4 hours or until the cake tests done.

Nutrition Information

- Calories: 578.4
- Sodium: 169.7
- Fiber: 0.6
- Sugar: 50.3
- Total Carbohydrate: 77.9
- Cholesterol: 149.3
- Total Fat: 27.4
- Saturated Fat: 13.1
- Protein: 6.8

---

155.   Strawberry Supreme Pound Cake

Serving: 7-10 serving(s) | Prep: 25mins | Ready in:

Ingredients

- 1 cup butter
- 1/2 cup shortening
- 2 3/4 cups sugar
- 6 large eggs
- 3 cups flour, sifted
- 1 teaspoon baking powder
- 3 teaspoons vanilla
- red food coloring
- 2 teaspoons strawberry flavoring
- 1 (10 ounce) package frozen strawberries, thawed
- Topping
- 1 (10 ounce) package strawberries
- red food coloring
- 1 1/2 cups powdered sugar
- 1 teaspoon almond flavoring
- 1/2 cup water

Direction

- Cream shortening, butter and sugar. Add eggs, one at a time, beating thoroughly after each one.
- Sift flour with baking powder; alternately add with strawberries. Add flavorings and food coloring.
- Pour batter into a greased and floured Bundt pan. Place in cold oven; turn on to 350° for approximately 1 1/2 hours. Remove cake from pan.
- Top with Strawberry Supreme Pound Cake Topping: Bring all ingredients to a simmer for 3 to 4 minutes. Apply to cake.

Nutrition Information

- Calories: 1058.8
- Fiber: 3.2
- Cholesterol: 251
- Protein: 11.7
- Total Fat: 45.9
- Saturated Fat: 21.7
- Sodium: 301.8
- Sugar: 108.3
- Total Carbohydrate: 152.8

---

156.   Sukkot Lemon Pound Cake

Serving: 8 serving(s) | Prep: 10mins | Ready in:

Ingredients

- 2 -3 tablespoons dairy-free margarine, melted (or non-dairy butter)
- 1/2 cup ground almonds
- 1 cup dairy-free margarine, at room temperature (or non-dairy butter)
- 1 2/3 cups sugar
- 5 eggs
- 1 1/2 tablespoons lemon juice
- 3 tablespoons lemon zest, grated

- 2 cups flour
- 1 teaspoon baking powder
- 1/2 teaspoon salt
- 1/4 cup powdered sugar (to garnish)
- 1 tablespoon lemon zest, grated, for garnish

Direction

- Preheat Oven to 325*F.
- (Prepare Pan).
- Brush bottom and sides of 9- by 5-inch loaf pan with melted margarine, dust with almonds and set aside.
- (Cake).
- Beat 1 cup margarine until soft and fluffy in bowl of electric mixer.
- Gradually add sugar and beat until light and creamy.
- Add eggs, 1 at a time, beating well after each addition.
- Beat in lemon juice and zest.
- Sift together flour, baking powder and salt and gradually stir into margarine mixture. Blend well.
- Pour batter into prepared pan and bake at 325 degrees until golden brown and toothpick inserted in center comes out clean, about 1 hour 10 minutes.
- Cool on wire rack.
- Slide knife around sides to loosen. Tip cake out of pan, set upright on rack and cool completely.
- Just before serving, sprinkle with powdered sugar and grated lemon zest.

Nutrition Information

- Calories: 372.3
- Sodium: 235.4
- Fiber: 1.9
- Cholesterol: 132.2
- Protein: 8.5
- Total Fat: 6.4
- Saturated Fat: 1.2
- Sugar: 46.1
- Total Carbohydrate: 71.5

157.   Sunny Citrus Pound Cake

Serving: 12 serving(s) | Prep: 15mins | Ready in:

Ingredients

- 2 3/4 cups sugar
- 1 cup butter
- 6 eggs
- 1 cup Greek yogurt or 1 cup sour cream
- 1/2 teaspoon lemon extract
- 1/2 teaspoon orange extract
- 1/2 teaspoon vanilla extract
- 2 lemons, zest of
- 3 cups flour
- 1/2 teaspoon fine sea salt or 1/2 teaspoon table salt
- 1/4 teaspoon baking soda
- Glaze
- 1/2 cup confectioners' sugar
- 2 lemons, juice of

Direction

- Preheat oven to 350°F Grease a 10" tube or Bundt pan.
- Cream butter and sugar in stand mixer with paddle attachment (or with hand mixer) until light and fluffy and pale in color. Add eggs, one at a time, beating to fully incorporate before adding the next. Beat in yogurt, extracts and lemon zest.
- Sift together flour, salt and baking soda. Add dry ingredients to wet, and stir until well-mixed.
- Pour batter into prepared pan and bake in the middle of the preheated oven, 60 minutes or until cake tester inserted in the middle of the cake comes out clean. Cool in pan 15 minutes, then turn out onto a rack to cool to room temperature.
- While cooling, stir together confectioner's sugar and lemon juice until smooth. Spoon

over cake once cool. Sprinkle with additional lemon zest while glaze is still wet, if desired.

Nutrition Information

- Calories: 486.3
- Total Fat: 18.1
- Sodium: 267.9
- Fiber: 0.9
- Sugar: 51.2
- Cholesterol: 146.4
- Protein: 6.6
- Saturated Fat: 10.5
- Total Carbohydrate: 75.6

| 158. | Sunshine Lemon Pound Cake |

Serving: 16 serving(s) | Prep: 15mins | Ready in:

Ingredients

- 2 1/2 cups flour
- 1 1/2 cups granulated sugar
- 1 tablespoon baking powder
- 1/2 teaspoon salt
- 4 eggs
- 3/4 cup orange juice
- 3/4 cup vegetable oil (or canola)
- 2 teaspoons lemon extract

Direction

- Preheat oven to 325; generously spray a 12-cup Bundt pan with cooking spray/baking spray; set aside.
- Mix all ingredients in large bowl.
- Beat with electric mixer on medium speed for 3 minutes.
- Pour into prepared pan.
- Bake 40-50 minutes or until toothpick inserted in center comes out clean.
- Remove from oven and let sit at least 30 minutes.

- Invert onto serving plate.
- Can be sliced warm but also cools very quickly.

Nutrition Information

- Calories: 258.8
- Saturated Fat: 1.8
- Sodium: 159.2
- Cholesterol: 46.5
- Total Fat: 11.6
- Fiber: 0.6
- Sugar: 19.8
- Total Carbohydrate: 35.2
- Protein: 3.7

| 159. | Super Rich Chocolate Pound Cake |

Serving: 10-12 serving(s) | Prep: 15mins | Ready in:

Ingredients

- 2 1/2 cups flour
- 3/4 cup unsweetened cocoa powder (I use Dutch processed)
- 1/2 teaspoon baking powder
- 1/2 teaspoon baking soda
- 1/2 teaspoon salt
- 1 cup butter, softened
- 2 cups sugar
- 4 large eggs, at room temperature
- 1 tablespoon vanilla extract
- 1 cup sour cream, at room temperature

Direction

- Preheat oven to 325*F.
- Grease and flour a 10" fluted tube pan.
- In a large bowl, whisk together the flour, cocoa powder, baking powder, baking soda, and salt; set aside.

- In another large bowl, using an electric mixer on high speed, cream the butter and sugar together until light and fluffy.
- Add the eggs, one at a time, beating well after each addition.
- Blend in the vanilla.
- In 3 additions each, beat in the flour mixture and sour cream just until combined.
- Do not overmix.
- Pour batter into the prepared pan.
- Bake for 60-70 minutes, or until the center tests done.
- Cool 10 minutes in pan; invert onto a wire rack and cool completely.

Nutrition Information

- Calories: 528.6
- Protein: 7.9
- Total Fat: 26.4
- Saturated Fat: 15.8
- Sodium: 370.4
- Total Carbohydrate: 68.7
- Fiber: 3
- Sugar: 40.5
- Cholesterol: 143.5

160.   The Best Crumb, Pound Cake Ever

Serving: 2 round cakes | Prep: 15mins | Ready in:

Ingredients

- 1/2 cup oil
- 1 tablespoon vanilla sugar
- 1/2 cup margarine
- 1 1/2 cups sugar
- 3 cups flour
- 2 tablespoons flat baking powder
- 4 large eggs
- 1 (8 ounce) container whipping cream (like Rich Whip)

Direction

- In a mixer with the beaters attached place; oil, vanilla sugar, margarine, sugar and flour.
- Mix on medium speed until coarse crumbs form.
- Remove 3/4 cup crumbs and set aside.
- To remaining crumbs in mixer add baking powder, eggs and whipping cream.
- Mix until smooth and creamy.
- Place in two 9-inch round aluminum pans or 1 9x 13 inch pan.
- Sprinkle crumbs on top.
- Bake at 350°F until ready 45-1 hour (or check; when a toothpick inserted in the middle comes out dry).

Nutrition Information

- Calories: 2695.6
- Total Carbohydrate: 300.8
- Cholesterol: 578.4
- Protein: 34.8
- Sugar: 151.3
- Total Fat: 153.6
- Saturated Fat: 45.5
- Sodium: 1807.9
- Fiber: 5.1

161.   Toasted Pound Cake With Cashew Caramel Sauce

Serving: 16 serving(s) | Prep: 8mins | Ready in:

Ingredients

- 50 caramels (one 14 oz. bag)
- 2/3 cup milk
- 1/2 cup cashew halves, and pieces
- 1 vanilla butter pound cake, cut into 16 slices

Direction

- Toast pound cake in toaster oven or conventional oven.
- Place caramels and milk in large microwavable bowl.
- Microwave on HIGH 3 - 3 1/2 minutes (or until caramels are completely melted and mixture is well blended), stirring after each minute.
- Stir cashews into caramel.
- Stir well before spooning 2 tablespoons over toasted pound cake.
- Eat quickly so no one else can get to it!

Nutrition Information

- Calories: 224.4
- Total Fat: 8.6
- Saturated Fat: 3.6
- Sugar: 20.9
- Total Carbohydrate: 35.3
- Cholesterol: 45.1
- Sodium: 184.3
- Fiber: 0.2
- Protein: 3.5

162. Traditional Pound Cake

Serving: 8-12 serving(s) | Prep: 30mins | Ready in:

Ingredients

- 3 cups cake flour
- 1/2 teaspoon baking powder
- 1 teaspoon salt
- 1 cup milk, room temperature
- 2 teaspoons vanilla
- 1 1/4 cups unsalted butter, softened
- 3 cups sugar
- 6 large eggs, room temperature

Direction

- Grease and flour a Bundt pan.

- In a bowl whisk the flour, baking powder, and salt together.
- In a bowl mix the milk and vanilla.
- In a bowl beat the butter and sugar together until it is light and fluffy. Beat in the eggs one at a time, until well combined.
- Add 1/3 of the flour, followed by half of the milk. Mix well.
- Then add another third of the flour, the second half of the milk. Mix well.
- Add the rest of the flour. Mix well.
- Pour batter into the pan.
- Tap the pan a few times on the counter to settle the batter.
- Place pound cake in the oven and turn the oven to 325 degrees.
- Let the cake cook, without opening the oven door, for 70 to 80 minutes.
- The cake is done once a wooden toothpick inserted into the middle comes out clean.
- Let the cake cool completely in the pan for.
- Use a small knife and cut around the edge of the cake to loosen it.
- Flip the cake upside down so that it come out of the pan.

Nutrition Information

- Calories: 806.9
- Total Carbohydrate: 117
- Cholesterol: 220
- Sugar: 75.3
- Protein: 10.2
- Total Fat: 33.9
- Saturated Fat: 20.1
- Sodium: 387.4
- Fiber: 0.9

163. Treva's Lemon Pound Cake

Serving: 8 serving(s) | Prep: 10mins | Ready in:

Ingredients

- 1 (18 ounce) box lemon cake mix (2 layer size)
- 1 (1 1/2 ounce) package instant lemon pudding mix (4 serving size)
- 4 eggs
- 1/2 cup oil
- 1 1/4 cups water

Direction

- Mix all ingredients in a large bowl with an electric mixer until blended.
- Pour batter into prepared tube pan.
- Bake at 350 for 50-60 minutes.
- Enjoy.

Nutrition Information

- Calories: 451.5
- Fiber: 0.7
- Total Carbohydrate: 54.7
- Saturated Fat: 3.9
- Sodium: 520.8
- Sugar: 27.8
- Cholesterol: 107
- Protein: 6
- Total Fat: 23.5

---

164. Triple Chocolate Pound Cake

Serving: 8-10 serving(s) | Prep: 25mins | Ready in:

Ingredients

- CAKE
- 14 tablespoons butter, softened
- 3 cups sugar
- 5 eggs
- 1 teaspoon vanilla extract
- 3 1/4 cups flour
- 1/2 cup unsweetened cocoa powder
- 1 teaspoon baking powder
- 1/2 teaspoon salt
- 1 1/3 cups milk
- 1 cup mini chocolate chip
- GLAZE
- 1 cup mini chocolate chip
- 2 tablespoons shortening
- 1 tablespoon light corn syrup

Direction

- CAKE: Preheat oven to 350*F.
- Grease and flour a 10" tube pan.
- With an electric mixer on low speed, cream together the butter and sugar.
- Add eggs, one at a time, blending well after each addition.
- Blend in vanilla.
- Scrape down sides of bowl; blend on high speed for 6 minutes, scraping bowl occasionally.
- Whisk together the flour, cocoa powder, baking powder, and salt.
- Mix in the flour mixture alternately with the milk, blending after each addition until the batter is smooth.
- Stir in the chocolate chips; pour batter into the prepared pan.
- Bake for 75-85 minutes, or until a toothpick tests done.
- Cool in pan for 20 minutes; invert onto a serving dish and cool completely.
- GLAZE: Combine the chocolate chips, shortening, and corn syrup in a saucepan over very low heat.
- Stir just until melted and smooth; cool slightly.
- Pour or spoon glaze over cake; let stand until glaze is set.

Nutrition Information

- Calories: 982.6
- Saturated Fat: 23.6
- Sodium: 406.2
- Fiber: 5.7
- Total Carbohydrate: 148.4
- Protein: 13.6

- Total Fat: 42.2
- Sugar: 99.8
- Cholesterol: 191.3

165.   Tropical Tasting Pound Cake

Serving: 1 bundt cake | Prep: 10mins | Ready in:

Ingredients

- 2 cups self rising flour
- 2 cups sugar
- 1 cup milk
- 1 cup oil
- 4 eggs
- 1 teaspoon rum flavoring
- 1 teaspoon coconut flavoring
- 1 teaspoon almond flavoring

Direction

- Mix dry ingredients.
- Stir in liquid ingredients mixing well.
- Pour into greased (or 'Pam' sprayed) Bundt pan.
- Bake @ 350 for 30-40 minutes or until toothpick comes out clean.
- A glaze can be added to the top if desired.

Nutrition Information

- Calories: 4822.2
- Saturated Fat: 40.4
- Sodium: 3582.9
- Total Carbohydrate: 598.5
- Total Fat: 248.4
- Sugar: 400.5
- Cholesterol: 778.2
- Protein: 57.9
- Fiber: 6.8

166.   Vanilla Bean Pound Cake

Serving: 10-12 serving(s) | Prep: 35mins | Ready in:

Ingredients

- 2 cups sugar (1 pound)
- 1/2 vanilla bean, used is fine
- 2 cups butter, at room temperature (1 pound)
- 9 large eggs (1 pound)
- 4 cups all-purpose flour (1 pound)
- 1 teaspoon salt
- 2 teaspoons vanilla extract

Direction

- Preheat oven to 325 degrees. In a food processor, grind vanilla bean and sugar until vanilla is as finely chopped as it can get, about one minute. Sift this mixture twice, making sure all larger pieces have been filtered out. Set aside.
- In a large bowl, cream the butter with an electric mixer, then gradually add the vanilla sugar, continuing to beat until well creamed and smooth. Add the eggs one at a time, beating well after each addition. Gradually add the flour and salt, beating constantly. Add the vanilla and lemon juice and continue beating until well blended.
- Grease and flour a 10-inch tube or Bundt pan. Pour in the batter and "spank" the bottom of the pan to distribute the batter evenly. Bake until a straw inserted into the cake comes out clean, about 1 hour 15 minutes, taking care not to overcook. Turn cake out onto a rack and let cool.

Nutrition Information

- Calories: 730.9
- Saturated Fat: 24.8
- Sodium: 558.1
- Fiber: 1.4
- Sugar: 40.6
- Total Carbohydrate: 78.6
- Cholesterol: 288

- Total Fat: 41.8
- Protein: 11.2

167. Vanilla Butternut Pound Cake With Maraschino Cherries

Serving: 1 cake | Prep: 20mins | Ready in:

Ingredients

- 1/2 cup shortening
- 1 cup margarine (2 sticks) or 1 cup butter (2 sticks)
- 1 teaspoon salt
- 2 cups sugar
- 5 large eggs
- 3 cups sifted flour
- 6 ounces evaporated milk
- 2 ounces water
- 1 cup chopped nuts
- 10 ounces maraschino cherries, well drained
- 2 tablespoons vanilla extract
- 2 teaspoons butter-nut flavoring, see note

Direction

- Cream shortening and butter until fluffy. Add sugar and salt. Beat in one egg at a time.
- Combine evaporated milk and water (to equal one cup total).
- Add flour and milk mixture alternately, ending with flour. Add flavorings, chopped nuts and the maraschino cherries.
- Pour batter into a greased and floured tube pan. Place cake in a cold oven. Bake at 325 degrees until done-.
- Remove cake from pan while still warm. Ice as desired.
- Note: The flavoring might be a bit difficult to find, but can be ordered online from the Superior Prod. Co. Charlotte N.C. as llangrove's review of Aug. 17th 2010 states. (Thank you llangrove for that information!).

Nutrition Information

- Calories: 6573.5
- Total Carbohydrate: 863
- Cholesterol: 979.3
- Total Fat: 304.9
- Saturated Fat: 70.3
- Sodium: 4869.8
- Sugar: 520.7
- Fiber: 31.5
- Protein: 107.1

168. Vanilla Marbled Pound Cake

Serving: 1 nine inch bundt cake, 12 serving(s) | Prep: 30mins | Ready in:

Ingredients

- 2 cups vanilla yogurt
- 4 cups flour
- 2 teaspoons baking soda
- 2 teaspoons baking powder
- 1 teaspoon salt
- 1/2 cup butter
- 2 cups sugar
- 4 eggs
- 1 tablespoon vanilla extract
- 1/2 cup unsweetened dutch process cocoa
- 1/2 cup milk semisweet chocolate chunks or 1/2 cup chocolate chips

Direction

- Combine flour, baking soda, baking powder, salt.
- Set aside.
- Beat butter sugar together until light fluffy.
- Add eggs, one at a time.
- Add vanilla.
- Alternately add flour mixture with the yogurt, ending with flour.
- Spoon about 2/3 of the batter into a lightly greased Bundt pan.

- Add cocoa powder to the remaining batter, mixing well.
- Stir in chocolate chunks.
- Drop chocolate batter over pan cut in with a knife.
- Bake in a preheated 350 degree over for one hour 15 minutes, or until cake tests done.
- Cool completely.

Nutrition Information

- Calories: 457.2
- Protein: 9
- Total Fat: 13.9
- Saturated Fat: 8.1
- Sodium: 576.2
- Sugar: 40.5
- Total Carbohydrate: 75.7
- Cholesterol: 87.9
- Fiber: 2.9

169. Vanilla Nut Sour Cream Pound Cake

Serving: 10 serving(s) | Prep: 10mins | Ready in:

Ingredients

- 2/3 cup butter, softened
- 2 cups sugar
- 2/3 cup sour cream
- 4 eggs
- 1 tablespoon vanilla
- 2 tablespoons liqueur (nut)
- 2 cups flour, sifted
- 1/2 teaspoon baking soda
- 1/4 cup confectioners' sugar (optional)

Direction

- Heat oven to 325 degrees. Grease and flour a 9-inch loaf pan.
- Beat butter, sugar and sour cream in large bowl with mixer on medium until light and

fluffy. Add eggs, 1 at a time, beating well after each addition. Mix in extract. Gradually beat in flour and baking soda on low speed.
- Pour batter into prepared pan. Bake 1 hour or until toothpick inserted in center comes out clean. Cool in pan 10 minutes. Remove from pan and cool on wire rack. Sprinkle with confectioners' sugar.

Nutrition Information

- Calories: 449.8
- Protein: 5.7
- Total Fat: 17.7
- Saturated Fat: 10.4
- Sodium: 187
- Fiber: 0.7
- Sugar: 40.4
- Total Carbohydrate: 60
- Cholesterol: 123.9

170. Virginia Pound Cake

Serving: 2 loaves | Prep: 20mins | Ready in:

Ingredients

- 1 lb butter
- 1 lb sugar
- 1 lb cake flour (4 cups)
- 10 eggs, separated
- 2 tablespoons brandy
- 1/4 teaspoon mace

Direction

- Preheat oven to 300°F and grease/flour two loaf pans.
- Cream butter, gradually add sugar, beating well after each addition.
- Beat egg whites to stiff peaks.
- Beat egg yolks until thick and lemon colored; add to creamed mixture.
- Add brandy.

- Sift flour and mace; add alternately with stiffly beaten egg whites.
- Pour into prepared pans and bake for 90 minutes.

Nutrition Information

- Calories: 3736.6
- Total Fat: 211
- Fiber: 3.9
- Sugar: 229.4
- Total Carbohydrate: 406.1
- Cholesterol: 1545.5
- Saturated Fat: 124.7
- Sodium: 1662.4
- Protein: 52

171.   Wet Chocolate L'orange Pound Cake

Serving: 1 Ten inch tube or Bundt pan, 16 serving(s) | Prep: 2hours30mins | Ready in:

Ingredients

- For Cake
- 3 cups granulated sugar
- 1 1/2 cups margarine or 1 1/2 cups butter, softened
- 3 cups all-purpose flour
- 1 (8 ounce) container sour cream
- 1 large idaho potato, cooked and mashed
- 1/2 cup unsweetened cocoa
- 1/2 cup orange juice
- 1 teaspoon baking soda
- 2 teaspoons orange extract
- 1/4 teaspoon salt
- 5 large eggs
- raspberries (to garnish)
- For Icing
- 1 (3 ounce) package cream cheese, softened
- 1 tablespoon milk
- 2 cups confectioners' sugar

- 1 teaspoon vanilla extract

Direction

- About 4 hours before serving or early in the day: preheat oven to 350°F.
- Grease and flour 10 inch tube or Bundt pan.
- In a large bowl, with mixer at low speed, beat sugar with margarine or butter just until blended.
- Increase speed to high, beat 3 minutes or until light and fluffy, scraping bowl often with rubber spatula.
- Reduce speed to low, add flour and next 8 ingredients; beat until well mixed, constantly scraping bowl.
- Increase speed to high, beat 2 minutes, occasionally scraping bowl.
- Spoon batter into prepared pan.
- Bake 1 hour and 30 minutes or until toothpick inserted in center of cake comes out clean.
- Cool cake in pan on wire rack 15 minutes.
- With spatula, loosen cake from pan, remove from pan and cool completely on rack.
- When cake is cool, prepare Cream Cheese Icing, spread on top of cake allowing some to drizzle down the sides of cake.
- Garnish cake with raspberries.
- To prepare the Cream Cheese Icing: In a small bowl, with mixer at low speed, beat softened cream cheese and milk until smooth.
- Beat in confectioners' sugar and vanilla extract until well-blended and a good spreading consistency, adding additional milk if necessary.

Nutrition Information

- Calories: 540.5
- Total Fat: 23.9
- Sugar: 53.9
- Total Carbohydrate: 77.8
- Cholesterol: 71.9
- Protein: 6.3
- Saturated Fat: 7
- Sodium: 369.4

- Fiber: 2

172. Whipped Pound Cake

Serving: 12-16 serving(s) | Prep: 50mins | Ready in:

Ingredients

- 1 cup butter
- 2 1/2 cups sugar
- 6 eggs
- 1/2 cup whipping cream
- 3 cups all-purpose flour
- 1 1/2 teaspoons vanilla

Direction

- Let the butter and eggs stand at room temperature for 30 minutes.
- Beat the butter and sugar with an electric mixer on medium to high speed until light and fluffy, about 10 minutes.
- Add the eggs, one at a time, beating 1 minute after each addition.
- Beat whipping cream until stiff peaks form.
- Add the flour and cream alternately to the egg mixture; beat just until combined after each addition.
- Beat in vanilla.
- Pour batter into a greased 10-inch tube pan. Bake in a 300 degree oven for 1 hours 15 minutes.
- Cool for 10 minutes on a wire rack. Remove cake from pan and cool thoroughly on wire rack.
- (Whipped cream substitute: 3/4 cup milk and 1/3 cup butter. Use amount required for recipe. Do this only for baking since this doesn't whip up like regular whipping cream.).

Nutrition Information

- Calories: 483.1
- Total Fat: 21.8
- Total Carbohydrate: 66
- Protein: 6.7
- Saturated Fat: 12.8
- Sodium: 148.4
- Fiber: 0.8
- Sugar: 42
- Cholesterol: 160

173. White Chocolate Pound Cake From Scratch

Serving: 12-16 serving(s) | Prep: 15mins | Ready in:

Ingredients

- 1 cup butter, softened
- 2 cups sugar
- 5 eggs
- 3 cups all-purpose flour
- 1/2 teaspoon baking soda
- 1/2 teaspoon baking powder
- 1/2 teaspoon salt
- 1 cup whole buttermilk
- 8 (1 ounce) squares white chocolate, melted

Direction

- Preheat oven to 300°. Grease and flour a 10-cup fluted tube pan.
- In a large bowl, beat butter and sugar at medium speed with an electric mixer until fluffy. Add eggs, one at a time, beating well after each addition.
- In a medium bowl, combine flour, baking soda, baking powder, and salt. Add to butter mixture alternately with buttermilk, beginning and ending with flour mixture, beating after each addition, just until combined. Stir in melted chocolate. Spoon batter into prepared pan.
- Bake for 1 hour 30 minutes, or until a wooden pick inserted in center comes out clean. Let cool in pan for 10 minutes. Remove from pan and let cool completely on a wire rack.

Nutrition Information

- Calories: 510.9
- Fiber: 0.8
- Cholesterol: 131.4
- Total Carbohydrate: 68.6
- Protein: 7.1
- Total Fat: 23.8
- Saturated Fat: 14.1
- Sodium: 320.2
- Sugar: 44.7

174. Wonderful Blueberry Pound Cake!

Serving: 1 (10-inch) tube cake | Prep: 10mins | Ready in:

Ingredients

- 2 1/4 cups sugar
- 1/2 cup butter, softened
- 4 ounces cream cheese, softened
- 3 large eggs
- 1 large egg white
- 3 cups flour, divided
- 2 cups blueberries (fresh or frozen, preferably fresh)
- 1 teaspoon baking powder
- 1/2 teaspoon baking soda
- 1/2 teaspoon salt
- 1 (8 ounce) carton lemon yogurt (low-fat is okay)
- 3 teaspoons vanilla
- 1 cup powdered sugar
- 2 tablespoons fresh lemon juice

Direction

- Set oven to 350°.
- Grease a 10-inch tube pan.
- In a bowl beat the sugar with butter and softened cream cheese until fluffy (about 5 minutes).
- Add in eggs and egg white one at a time until blended.
- Add in the vanilla.
- In a small bowl toss the blueberries with 2 tablespoons flour (removed from the 3 cups flour) set aside.
- In another bowl mix the remaining flour with baking powder, baking soda and salt; add to the creamed mixture along with the yogurt, beginning and ending with the flour.
- Fold in the blueberry mixture.
- Transfer the mixture prepared tube pan.
- Bake for about 1 hour and 10 minutes or until cake tests done.
- Cool cake 10 minutes in pan then remove.
- In a small bowl combine the powdered sugar with lemon juice, then drizzle over warm cake.

Nutrition Information

- Calories: 5465
- Protein: 83
- Fiber: 17.2
- Cholesterol: 1012.4
- Sugar: 644.5
- Total Carbohydrate: 950.9
- Total Fat: 153.8
- Saturated Fat: 90.1
- Sodium: 3554.9

175. Yummy Low Fat Chocolate Chip Pound Cake

Serving: 1 cake, 16 serving(s) | Prep: 20mins | Ready in:

Ingredients

- 1 package chocolate cake mix (dark or milk, non-fat is good)
- 1 package instant chocolate pudding mix
- 1/2 cup applesauce
- 1/2 cup water
- 4 Egg Beaters egg substitute (or other egg substitute)

- 1 (12 ounce) package chocolate chips
- confectioners' sugar

Direction

- Mix all ingredients except the eggs, chocolate and confectioners' sugar.
- Add eggs one at a time.
- Beat well with a mixer.
- Fold in the chocolate chips.
- Spray Pam on a Bundt pan and pour in the mixture.
- Bake for one hour at 350 degrees F.
- Cool for about twenty minutes and unmold.
- Sift confectioners' sugar over the top.
- (Sugar optional) Do not refrigerate.

Nutrition Information

- Calories: 271.4
- Sugar: 27.3
- Total Carbohydrate: 44.3
- Protein: 3
- Total Fat: 11.6
- Sodium: 363.3
- Fiber: 2.4
- Cholesterol: 0
- Saturated Fat: 4.9

Index

A

Almond 3,7,23,32,34

Apple 3,4,50,58,83,93

Apricot 3,4,9,90,92

B

Baking 11,57

Banana 3,11,12

Berry 70

Blueberry 3,4,5,16,60,113

Bran 3,4,9,85

Butter
3,4,5,11,20,25,27,37,42,49,50,51,52,53,54,56,83,85,89,109

C

Cake
1,3,4,5,6,7,8,9,10,11,12,13,14,15,16,17,18,19,20,21,22,23,2
4,25,26,27,28,29,30,31,32,33,34,35,36,37,38,39,40,41,42,4
3,44,45,46,47,48,49,50,51,52,53,54,55,56,57,58,59,60,61,6
2,63,64,65,66,67,68,69,70,71,72,73,74,75,76,77,78,79,80,8
1,82,83,84,85,86,87,88,89,90,91,92,93,94,95,96,97,99,100,
101,102,103,104,105,106,107,108,109,110,111,112,113

Caramel 3,4,5,11,79,80,90,105

Cardamom 3,20

Cashew 5,105

Cheese 3,4,11,24,25,27,33,37,38,69,72,87,111

Cherry 3,15,22

Chicken 3,23

Chocolate
3,4,5,14,23,24,25,26,27,28,29,30,41,48,52,59,70,71,86,92,9
6,104,107,111,112,113

Cider 3,50

Cinnamon 3,31,32,59

Cocktail 3,46

Coconut 3,4,31,34,40,60,80

Coffee 3,20

Cranberry 3,4,36,37,77,91

Cream
3,4,5,6,7,9,11,12,13,16,17,18,22,24,25,27,28,33,34,36,37,3
8,39,44,45,47,48,50,55,56,58,65,72,73,74,75,77,85,86,87,8
8,95,96,97,101,102,103,109,110,111

Curd 3,4,43,52

E

Egg 11,22,113

F

Fat
5,6,7,8,9,10,11,12,13,14,15,16,17,18,19,20,21,22,23,24,25,
26,27,28,29,30,31,32,33,34,35,36,37,38,39,40,41,42,43,44,
45,46,47,48,49,50,51,52,53,54,55,56,57,58,59,60,61,62,63,
64,65,66,67,68,69,70,71,72,73,74,75,76,77,78,79,80,81,82,
83,84,85,86,87,88,90,91,92,93,94,95,96,97,98,99,100,101,1
02,103,104,105,106,107,108,109,110,111,112,113,114

Flour 11,58,94

Fruit 3,4,46,47,52,53,92

Fudge 3,29

G

Gin 3,4,39,48,49,61,90

H

Hazelnut 3,4,26,54

Honey 4,55

I

Icing 3,4,23,29,59,90,96,111

J

Jus 38,52,92,103

Conclusion

Thank you again for downloading this book!

I hope you enjoyed reading about my book!

If you enjoyed this book, please take the time to share your thoughts and post a review on Amazon. It'd be greatly appreciated!

Write me an honest review about the book – I truly value your opinion and thoughts and I will incorporate them into my next book, which is already underway.

Thank you!

If you have any questions, **feel free to contact at:** *author@hugecookbook.com*

Tori Ramos

hugecookbook.com

Made in the USA
Columbia, SC
19 March 2024

33341013R00065